In the Footsteps of Reivers

Brian Dingle

In the Footsteps of Reivers

Olympia Publishers
London

First Published in 2017
Olympia Publishers

60 Cannon Street
London
EC4N 6NP

Printed in Great Britain

Contents

Introduction	19
The Marches and Debatable Lands	23
The English East March	23
The English Middle March	25
English West March	27
Scottish East March	29
Scottish Middle March	31
Scottish West March	33
The Debatable Lands	35
Names and Nicknames	37
Religion and the Reivers	40
Rodes, Trods and Dogs	45
Truce Days	48
The Wardens	51
Food for Thought	54
Dressing the Part	57
Armed and Dangerous	59
Passing the Time	64
Brinkburn Priory	68
Dryburgh Abbey	70
Hexham Abbey	72
Jedburgh Abbey	74
Kelso Abbey	76
Lanercost Priory	78
Lindisfarne Priory	80
Melrose Abbey	83
Sweetheart Abbey	85
Other Border Abbeys and Priories	87
Alnwick Abbey	87

Blanchland Abbey   87
Coldingham Priory   87
Hulne Friary   88
Wetheral Priory   88

The Battle of Ancrum Moor   89
27 January 1545   89
The Battle of Arkinholme   92
1 May 1455   92
The Battle of Dryfe Sands   94
6 December 1593   94
Battle of Flodden Field   98
9 September 1513   98
The Battle of Halidon Hill   104
19 July 1333   104
Hell Beck (Gelt)   108
20 February 1570   108
The Battle of Homildon Hill   110
14 September 1402   110
The Battle of Otterburn   114
5 August 1388   114
The Battle of Pinkie Cleugh   119
10 September 1547   119
The Raid of the Redeswire   124
7 July 1575   124
The Battle of Solway Moss   127
24 November 1542   127
Other Border Battles   129

    Duns (1372)   129
    Hadden Rig (24 August 1542)   129
    Melrose (25 July 1526)   129
    Millerton Hill (1467)   130
    Nisbet Moor (22 June 1402)   130
    Roxburgh, The Siege of (3 August 1460)   131
    Sark (23 October 1448)   131
    Yeavering (22 July 1415)   131

Akeld Bastle   132

"The Little Fortlet"   132
Alnwick Castle   134
"The Windsor of the North"   134
Ancroft Vicars Pele   139
Aydon Castle   142
"A Converted Manor"   142
Bamburgh Castle   145
"Castle of Kings"   145
Barmoor Castle   147
"The Rest before Flodden"   147
Berwick Castle   149
"The Forgotten One"   149
Berwick's Elizabethan Walls   152
Bewcastle Castle   154
Black Middens Bastle   156
"Fortified Farmhouse"   156
Brough Castle   158
"Clifford's Retreat"   158
Brougham Castle   162
Carlisle Castle   165
"Buccleuch Dares, Kinmont Wins"   165
Chillingham Castle   170
Corbridge Vicars Pele   173
Dunstanburgh Castle   175
"Lancaster's Jewel in the North"   175

Edlingham Castle   178

Edlingham Tower   180
Embleton Vicars Pele   181
Etal Castle   183
"To the Manners Born"   183
Ford Castle   186
Lindisfarne Castle   189
"The Guardian of the Holy Isle"   189
Naworth Castle   191
Norham Castle   193
"Castle of the Prince Bishops"   193
Penrith Castle   197

"A Castle fit for Kings"	197
Preston Tower	199
"Half a Castle"	199
Prudhoe Castle	201
"Never Taken by the Scots"	201
Thirlwall Castle	205
"Nicely Tucked Away"	205
Twizel Castle	207
"Above the Bridge"	207
Warkworth Castle	209
"The Lion of the North"	209
Woodhouses Bastle	213
"The Strong Pele"	213
Other English Fortifications	215
Caerlaverock Castle	222
"Maxwell's Castle of the Skylark"	222
Cessford Castle	225
"The Small Tough One"	225
Dryhope Tower	227
"The Flower of Yarrow"	227
Fast Castle	229
"Castle on an Island"	229
Fatlips Castle	231
"Turnbulls on the Hill"	231
Ferniehirst Castle	233
"Scotland's Alamo"	233
Gilnockie Tower	236
"Home of Black Jock"	236
Greenknowe Tower	238
"Setons Retreat"	238
Hermitage Castle	240
"The Strength of Liddesdale"	240
Home (Hume) Castle	243
Kirkhope Tower	245
Langholm Castle	247
"Armstrong's Last Ride"	247
Lochmaben Castle	249
"Started by Bruce, finished by Edward"	249
Lochwood Tower	252

Morton Castle	255
Neidpath Castle	257
Queen Mary's House	260
Repentance Tower	262
Roxburgh Castle	265
Smailholm Tower	267
Threave Castle	269
"The Grim's Seat"	269
Torthorwald Castle	271
"Constant Change"	271
Other Scottish Fortifications	274
The Raid and Capture of Geordie Burns	280
"The Confessions of a Reiver"	280
Hobbie Noble	282
"An English Reiver amongst the Armstrongs"	282
Johnnie Armstrong	285
"Murder at the Hands of a King"	285
The Rescue of Kinmont Willie	289
April 16th 1596	289
Lang Sandy Armstrong	293
The Tall One is Hanged"	293
The Tale of Muckle Mouth Meg	296
"The Hangman or a Wife"	296
Richie Graham	299
"The Blackmailer Extraordinaire"	299
Sir John Carmichael	303
(1542-1600)	303
"A better Englishman than a Scotsman"	303
Sir John Forster	306
(1502-1602)	306
"The Old Rogue"	306
Sir Robert Carey	309
(1560-1639)	309
"The Courtier"	309
Sir Robert Ker	312
(1570-1650)	312
"The Fyrebrand"	312
Lord Bothwell and Wee Jock of the Park	316
"How to lose a castle"	316

Union of the Crowns and Ill Week 318
Armstrongs Goodnight 322
Glossary 323
Further Reading 328

Introduction

It's been over 400 years since the time of the reivers, one of the most forgotten times in British history. As times and areas go it was one of the most violent anywhere in the world and at any time in history.

Before the end of the thirteenth century the English-Scottish Border was a peaceful and relatively wealthy area with the port of Berwick on the ascendancy. Sheep farmers from the Merse, the fertile area of land to the north west of Berwick sent their fleeces to Berwick to be sold abroad in exchange for other goods, life was good for the borderer on both sides. There appeared to be little animosity, in fact to a lot of people on either side of the Border, the Border might as well not been there. Scottish and English lords and earls had owned lands on both sides of the Border.

The peace in the Border was about to be broken in a way that would take over 300 years to restore. The death of Alexander III of Scotland in 1286 sent shock waves through the kingdom; he had been a popular king and had left Scotland in a prosperous state. Alexander died without leaving an heir to the throne; both of his sons had died before him. Whilst there were no direct descendants there were, however claimants to the throne.

Initially Alexander was succeeded by his daughter Margaret who had married Eric the King of Norway. Unfortunately their daughter, Margaret died in 1290 on her way to Scotland from Norway. As Margaret and Eric only had daughters, this again left the throne open. The two main claimants to the throne were John Balliol and Robert the Bruce, 5th Lord Annandale.

The Reivers statue in Galashiels, a testament to the past on both sides of the border.

John Balliol was descended from David I of Scotland although his family held lands in County Durham, most notably Barnard Castle. His father John was the 5th Lord of Barnard Castle. Balliol's main competitor for the crown, Robert the Bruce the 5th Lord Annandale also had the title of Lord Hartlepool proving both claimants had lands in England. Bruce was also descended from David I and was the grandfather of the Robert the Bruce, who would become King of Scots in 1306.

Both men handed their claims into the Scottish auditors, the main arbitrator for this task being Edward I of England. The ruling was in favour of Balliol and he was duly crowned at Scone Palace near Stirling. Edward viewed Balliol as subservient to himself and someone that could be manipulated, demanding that Balliol pay homage to him. However that wasn't the way things happened and the Scots, tired of the treatment from Edward and determined that Balliol's reign should end as his position was undermined by Edward. A council of twelve of Scotland's lords met at Stirling in 1295 and signed the Treaty of Mutual Assistance with France that would become known as the "the Auld Alliance".

The result was that a displeased Edward invaded Scotland in 1296, starting the first War of Scottish Independence. This was the struggle for Scotland to remain independent and England trying to assert its authority like a big brother over a smaller but stubborn sibling. The borders then became a battleground that lasted over 300 years until after the Union of the Crowns in 1603.

Living in any war zone develops a hard and resilient breed of people; they have to survive by living off what they can find. This could be stealing, by force if necessary, and in the Anglo-Scottish borders during the thirteenth to sixteenth centuries that was commonplace and increased as time went by. The violence rose slowly, forged by a background of war, where both sides fought over the border ground and the independence of Scotland. Alongside this warfare the strength of the people grew, forming their own laws and customs, as well as the fortresses to protect them and their valuable livestock. Thus began the rise of the reivers where family loyalty and strength came before country loyalty. Some families had branches on both sides of the Border, so alliances between families and also feuds between families became common. With these came the events, tales and characters that gave the borders such a rich history.

The borders on both sides were split into three marches, this was for governance as well as military purposes, each march had its own warden and deputy warden to oversee law and order, probably one of the hardest jobs in the borders and certainly one of the most thankless. Over all the wardens was a Lord Warden of the Marches.

This was indeed a lawless society and families on both sides of the Border fought with one another and rode with each other. Their names became synonymous with the border reivers, names like Charlton, Robson, Milburn and Graham on the English side and Armstrong, Elliot, Bell, Maxwell, Scott and Johnstone on the Scottish side. With the increase in the raiding and the feuds came the strong houses and the towers to protect the families of the wealthier. The bastle houses seen mainly on the English side of the Border take their name from the French Bastilles meaning fort, although it was in fact a prison. On the Scottish side towers called Peel or Pele from the word Palisade, like Gilnockie, line up along the border.

The reivers also left their mark in the dictionary, with words like blackmail and bereaved still in use today. As fighting men and light cavalry there were none better, as disciplined soldiers possibly not so. In an area where courage, strength and living on your wits were needed in abundance, successive monarchs from both sides of the borders used these men in times of war. When there was no war they kept in trim fighting amongst themselves.

Whichever way you view them – villain, hero, gentry, or cattle thief and soldier – you cannot but be in awe of what they left behind in the fortifications, the stories of battles and tales of the area and of its people. A rich legacy indeed for one and all to enjoy in our, more peaceful times.

The Marches and Debatable Lands

The English East March

The smallest of the English marches stretched from Berwick-upon-Tweed in the north to the Waren Burn just north of Alnwick in the south, although after 1580 this had stretched south to the River Aln, just north of Alnwick. Then from the North Sea to the eastern side of the Cheviot Hills. This took in the areas of Norhamshire, the lands around the village of Norham on the south bank of the Tweed and Islandshire, the Island of Lindisfarne and the mainland lands adjacent to the Island which were controlled by the Priory on the Island. These lands were controlled by the see or palatinate of Durham. The control for the East March was at Berwick Castle.

Along with Berwick, this March also had the magnificent castles of Bamburgh, Lindisfarne, Dunstanburgh, and Chillingham, as well as the castles of Etal, Ford, Norham and Wark. The castles of Berwick, Norham and Wark bore the brunt of the raids being the ones lying on the Border with Scotland. Numerous pele towers and bastle house are scattered through the area, the area of Wooler and Glendale have a number of bastle houses, one of the most notable being Akeld. It also contains one of the most important battle sites of the Tudor period, Flodden Field.

The noted 'reiving names', also known as riding names for the East March were the Selbys, the Greys, the Herons, the Dunns and the Forsters, of whom that old rogue Sir John Forster is probably the most notable.

The keep of Norham castle on the southern banks of the Tweed

The English Middle March

The Middle March stretched from the Cheviots in the east to the Bewcastle Waste in the west. With the Cheviots as its eastern boundary and the Border with Scotland was the northern border, the southern border went down to Durham, actually in some parts stretching south of the River Tyne. This March was controlled from Alnwick Abbey, situated near the castle and took in most of the towns of southern Northumberland including Hexham, Morpeth and Newcastle. It also contained the notorious reiving valleys of Tynedale and Redesdale. In fact the Middle March was almost all of Northumberland except for its north-eastern quarter.

The March contained the castles of Alnwick, Morpeth, Newcastle, Harbottle, Warkworth and Thirlwall. It contained the first purpose-built gaol in the country at Hexham. The notable reiving families of the March were the Robsons, the Charltons, the Halls, the Hedleys and the Rutherfords.

The 14th century gatehouse, all that remains of Alnwick Abbey

English West March

This was the counties of Cumberland and Westmorland, although during the reiving times the southern end of Westmorland was relatively untouched. Stretching in the north-west to the Solway Firth, in the north-east it stretched into what was known as the Debatable lands, which also bordered the Scottish west and middle marches. In the south the Border was Lancashire and Yorkshire. In the east the border was the English Middle March of Northumberland.

The wardens' base was at Carlisle Castle, although in earlier times Richard of Gloucester, who became Richard III, preferred Penrith Castle as he had this modified while he owned it during his wardenry between 1471 and 1478. The March included the castles at Carlisle, Triermain, Askerton and at Bewcastle where it watched over the reivers' thoroughfare of Bewcastle waste. Further south the castles of Brough, Brougham, Penrith and Appleby protected what we would now call the A66 corridor, but was then a route into Scotland from south to north.

This March had some notable reiving names, among them the Grahams, the Storeys, the Musgraves, the Lowthers, the Salkelds and the Nobles.

Carlisle Castle, the base for the control of the English west March

Scottish East March

This is basically the county of Berwickshire, immediately north of Berwick-upon-Tweed, to the Lammermuir Hills, and from the North Sea to just east of Kelso. The southern border was generally the River Tweed and the English Border. It is the smallest of the Scottish marches, but contained the very important fertile land called The Merse. This was from Coldingham near the coast to Duns and then south to Berwick and the River Tweed. It was important for the sheep farming and wool production that had made this area of Scotland one of the richest in the country prior to the reiving period and the envy of England.

The March wardens were generally the Hume (Home) family who controlled the March from either Home Castle or Fast Castle. The Scottish east March only had one town, this was Eyemouth, situated in the south-east corner of the March and only a few miles north of Berwick its counterpart in the English East March.

The notable reiving families in the East March were the Humes or Homes, the Dixons, the Cranstons and the Trotters.

Home Castle near Kelso, the main castle of the Home family who controlled the Scottish East March.

Scottish Middle March

This March was probably the most troublesome, both for the Scottish themselves and to the English across the Border. As it included the lonely valley of Liddesdale and the north-west side of the Debatable Lands. This gave a constant source of trouble from probably the largest family in the borders, the Armstrongs.

The Middle March stretches from just east of Kelso to just west of Kershopefoot in the west. To the north it stretched past the town of Peebles in Tweeddale and to the south the Tweed and Liddel Water and the English Border.

This included the sherrifdoms of Peebles, Roxburgh and Selkirk. It also included a substantial number of towns including Roxburgh which now is just a memory, others that still stand today are Hawick, Selkirk, Peebles, Galashiels, Melrose and Jedburgh.

It also had a good supply of castles for protection including Hermitage, Cessford, Ferniehirst and Neidpath. All of them had their fair share of action against the Auld Enemy, being burnt or besieged at some point during the fourteenth to sixteenth centuries.

The noted names in the Middle March struck fear anywhere in the borders, including the Armstrongs, the Elliots, the Pringles, the Kers, the Scotts, the Burns and the Turnbulls. The March was controlled by the current march warden's place of residence. If the Kers had the wardenship it would be controlled from either Ferniehirst or Cessford. The valley of Liddesdale had its own warden, the "Keeper of Liddesdale". This was controlled exclusively from Hermitage Castle, though exactly how much effect this had on the reivers and enforcing law and order is open to debate.

Ferniehirst Castle, home and powerbase to one branch of the Kerr family.

Scottish West March

Almost as much trouble to the two crowns as the Scottish and English middle marches, the West March stretched from the edge of the Debatable Lands in the east to the River Cree in the west. With the Liddel Water and River Sark forming its boundary with England and then the Solway Firth, this March was in principle controlled from Dumfries Castle. In practise, however, it too was controlled from the seat of the family holding the wardenship at the time. If the Maxwells held sway then it would be controlled from Caerlaverock Castle, if the Johnstones had the wardenship then they would control it from Lochwood Tower.

The West March had a number of towns all much the same size although smaller than Dumfries, these included Kirkcudbright in the west to Langholm in the east as well as Annan and Lockerbie. It is also the home of the battle site of the largest family battle in border history, that of Dryfe Sands near Lockerbie.

Noted reiver names from the West March include the Maxwells, the Johnstones, the Bells, the Irvines, the Moffats and the Carruthers. There was of course a smattering of Armstrongs and Elliots within the March. Religion had a place here with the Abbey of Sweetheart just south-west of Dumfries.

Threave Castle, built by Archibald "The Grim" Douglas.

The Debatable Lands

These stretch from present-day Metal Bridge on the River Esk in the south to Gretna in the north, about four miles, then north-easterly to Tarras Moss a distance of some ten miles, making some forty square miles. Whilst small and crossing the border around present-day Canonbie it is of some significance in the tales and history of the border reivers. Fully claimed by neither England nor Scotland, it was in effect a lawless land.

Neither side could blame the other for the problems within the area. In the north of the area it was inhabited by the Armstrongs and the Elliots, to the south the Grahams. As it became more lawless it became the sanctuary, if that is the right word for it, for broken men and those who had been put to the horn[1]. With the area filling with thieves, murderers, and other vagabonds, this led to the area being described as "a nest of vipers".

It became necessary for both countries to act, as neither could claim ownership of the area and each blamed the other for the reiving that went on from the area. In 1551 a commission was set up to look at the area and the problem, however to nobody's surprise there was no agreement. Whilst there was no agreement on the division of the land they did issue a joint edict that "Any Englishman or Scotsman shall be free to rob, burn, spoil, slay, murder and destroy all and such person or persons, their bodies, buildings goods and cattle as do remain or shall inhabit upon any part of the said Debatable Land, without any redress to be made to the same". So it was business as usual for the reivers, with the edict most probably stoking the fire.

The situation got intolerable and in 1552 the French Ambassador was asked to arbitrate by both countries, in itself a step forward. In true diplomatic fashion, he decided that the border should be straight down the middle. This led to the building of an earthwork mound we know as Scots Dyke. It was marked with border stones and today with a small bridge and

---

[1]Men who had been disowned by their families

wooden marker. However this didn't have any real effect on the reivers within the Debatable Lands, or for that matter in any of the other marches.

The marker for Scots Dyke, with the original marker stone is shown though the line gap.

Names and Nicknames

St Mary's Loch where many a Reiver passed by.

Names in the borders were at the very fabric of society; they meant everything to the families and the members of them. In the borders there weren't clans but families or graynes, this led to the phrase of "to go with the grayne" meaning to go with your family, as opposed to being linked to wood working. To lose your name or to be cast out by your family and become a "broken man" or be "put to the horn". This was the ultimate disgrace, since their names bonded them together.

In the beginning there were no surnames only given names. However later it became necessary for people to have surnames for differentiation, often taking the form of where the person came from such as "John of Charlton" became John Charlton, or "James from Douglas" would become James Douglas.

However, in the borders the number of forenames didn't appear to have a large pool, the same names would appear again and again. Common ones would be William Armstrong, Andrew Kerr, Richie Graham, William Tait or John Elliot. Sons had the names of their fathers and in some circumstances second sons had the same name, if the older sibling had died before they were born. This not only confused their families but others, including the courts as well.

To get over this lack of inventiveness on the naming of their offspring, they were very inventive with the nicknames or "To-names" they gave them. These could take the form of where they came from as in the case of Wee Jock of the Park, who was John Elliot of the Park Farm or Auld Wat of Harden, who was Walter Scott from Harden near Hawick.

Who someone's father was could be one way of differentiating their names, as in Laird's Jock or Laird's Wat, who could be the Hedesman's sons John and Walter. If the father was dead or not around, such as when the couple had split after handfasting, then it could be the mother's name that would be used, as in Katie's Sim who was Simon, Katie's son.

This could also extend to a person's sexuality as in George Buggerback Elliot, or Davy the Lady Armstrong who was Sim the "Lairds brother," an important position in border society. This was in no way a detraction, as their sexuality was accepted within border society.

Another way someone could be named was with regards to a part of their anatomy, as in the case of Nebless Clem Crozier, who most probably lost his nose in a sword fight or an accident. There was rarely anything malicious in the names, only a way of telling people apart.

These nicknames were also written into court documents to distinguish between numerous Walter Scotts or Jock Elliots.

The Millholm Cross, as lasting monument to the Armstrong family.

Religion and the Reivers

In the three hundred years that the reivers were riding the border hills, the main religion was Roman Catholics. Only in the sixteenth century, after 1530 and the Protestant Reformation took hold, did that change. For the most part the Reivers didn't care much for any religion. It was an area where there were few churches at that time and even fewer priests, and priests routinely wore swords for their own protection. And often what churches there were had Pele towers built either onto them or nearby for the protection of the clergy.

The lack of priests also had an effect on the parishioners, who had to wait to get married or christened if there was no priest in the vicinity. With christenings this wasn't so much of a problem as they could wait until a priest was passing. Weddings however were different these had to be organised even in the fourteenth to sixteenth centuries. So what happened is that couples would live together before a priest was found, which could be for up to a year depending on how remote the community was. This living together was called "handfasting" and it was an accepted part of border life. Any children born within this period would be taken care of and treated as if they had been born within the marriage. When the priest was next in their village the wedding ceremony would take place and all children would then be encompassed into the family. On rare occasions the couple would split up before a priest could be found, in which instance the children were still taken care of as if they were full family members.

The statue of St Cuthbert near Lindisfarne Priory, looking towards the castle.

Reivers were universally hated not only by the governments of both England and Scotland for their law violations, but also by the church in both countries. In England the reivers of Tynedale appeared to have special mention from Cardinal Wolsey and also Richard Fox the Prince Bishop of Durham. In Scotland the reivers of Liddesdale came in for special mention in 1525 from the Archbishop of Glasgow, Gavin Dunbar, who announced a curse the reivers delivered from his pulpit. The good Archbishop knew how to curse. His sermon took fully forty-five minutes to deliver the damning indictment on the reivers, some of which follows:

"… I curse thair heid and all the haris of the thair heid; I curse their face, thair een, thair mooth, thair neise, thair toung, thair crag, thair shoulderis, thair breist, thair hert, thair stomok, thair bak, thair wame, thair airmes, thair leggis, thair handis, thair feit, and everilk pairt of thair body, frae the top of thair heid tae the soill of thair feit, before and behind, within and withoot…"

The curse probably had no effect on the reivers. They carried on their business with undiminished enthusiasm in fact Sim Armstrong of Whithaugh responded to the curse and the excommunication of the reivers by burning thirty churches in the borders.

The priests who did administer in the borders were often illiterate and strove to do a hard job with criticism from not only the reivers but from the established church and those higher up the ecclesiastical circles, which were almost always intertwined with the politics of the day. Often these priests would wander through the countryside preaching as they went, whether it was in a church or at a market cross. They were known as "Book a Bosom" priests, owing to them keeping their Bible and communion artefacts inside their robes.

The cursing stone, by artist Gordon Young is situated in the walkway between The Castle and the Tullie House Museum in Carlisle

One such priest who wandered the borders administering to reiver families throughout Northumberland trying to meet the families on their own terms was Bernard Gilpin, often called "the Reivers' priest" or "the Apostle of the North". Born in Kentmere in what was Westmorland, though he was the parish priest in Houghton le Spring in County Durham. Bernard, unlike some of his contemporaries, was an educated man, having studied at Oxford. In spite of this he met the people on their own terms giving comfort to all. By all accounts he was well received by the people, in that they didn't try to kill him, which is what they most probably would have done with some of the church hierarchy.

Bernard's ministering didn't go down well with Queen Mary since he was a noted Protestant. Bernard, having gone to Europe soon after Queen Mary took the throne of England in 1553, returned in 1556 to the rectory of Easington in County Durham. Edmund Bonnor, advisor to Queen Mary, issued a royal warrant for Gilpin. However on his way to London, and what would have been certain death by fire, Gilpin fell and broke his leg. Whilst recovering from this, Queen Mary died and England returned to the Protestant religion under Elizabeth I, which was instrumental in saving Gilpin's Life.

It could be said that despite Bernard Gilpin and other priests' best efforts, and all the cursing and threats by higher members of ecclesiastical society, that the borders was a religious void as demonstrated by the tale of a visitor to Liddesdale in the Debatable lands who wondered what religion was worshipped in the area as he couldn't find any churches. Not to be thwarted, he asked a local if there were any Christians around. The borderer replied he didn't know if there were any and that in that area, they were all Elliots and Armstrongs, a reference to two names of the most numerous families in the area during the sixteenth century.

Rodes, Trods and Dogs

If a person had been raided or relieved of his goods or been "spoyled" as it was more commonly known in a raid, he had a number of options open to him. The first would be to report the matter to his warden in the hope that it would be dealt with at the next truce day. However these were often few and far between and largely depended upon who was the warden on each side. There was also no guarantee his bill would be read at that truce day.

The next option would be to pursue the raiders and goods immediately in the form of a trod, if the pursuit was taken immediately after the raid, on the same night or within twenty-four hours then it was known as a "hot trod". This would be done on horseback or on foot and the pursuit often required the use of a tracking dog called a sleuth or slewe hound.

The Bloodhound, used as a slewe Hound on a trod to track Reivers.

One of the party carried a flaming torch denoting the trod and giving it the name "Hot Trod".

The final option would be to mount a pursuit after a period of time had elapsed, after the first twenty-four hours but inside six days from the day of spoyling, this was known as the "cold trod". It followed the same principle and rules as the hot trod, just that there had been more time elapsed before the pursuing party set off.

The person spoyled would gather together family, friends and neighbours to assist him on the trod. It was unknown for someone to refuse to go on a lawful trod as the punishment before 1550 was death. This was then mitigated to seven days in prison and a fine of 3s 4d, a not inconsiderable sum in the middle of the sixteenth century, also they were due a percentage of the recovered goods. This amounted to 1d in the pound for goods that were recovered in England and one penny in the pound for those recovered in Scotland.

Both countries recognised the legality of the trod, the main criteria to make this legal was once they had crossed the Border, they had to inform the first person they met or the first village they came to that it was a trod and that they were in pursuit. The trod would have been an impressive sight, with the flaming peat on a lance as the torch at the front and with hounds baying and the sounding of horns, it gave rise to the phrase "with hue and cry".

The trod had the legal ability to mete out justice if the reivers were caught in possession of the goods; this also gave rise to the phrase to be caught "red handed". However sometimes the tables were turned and the reivers, after hiding their booty, would lie in wait for the trod. Needless to say, that death during the fight was commonplace.

The thought that the pursuing trod would catch the reivers quickly if they set off in pursuit soon after the raid would have been thought the most likely outcome, especially if the reivers were driving sheep or, even more slowly, moving pigs. However the Reivers knew their way over the mosses and other boggy places as well as tracks unknown to others and could arrive safely at their chosen destination without being caught.

The trod should not be confused with a warden rode. This was organised by the march warden as a foray into another march to recover goods. As often as not the men accompanying him would be in his service and be obliged to go. It was equally as dangerous as the trod and fray and death were not uncommon. Some wardens invented stories and set up rodes to be able to raid on the other side of the Border. Others on the rode were entitled to a share of all the recovered goods.

In both the warden rode and the hot and cold trod the use of the sleuth hound or slewe hound was commonplace. These dogs were bred to follow a trail, along with speed and stamina; they were often taken on raids if the opportunity arose. The dogs, like bloodhounds and limers were well looked after, better often than some people. The limer has died out, unfortunately. They would also be used for hunting as they could track for deer or wild cattle.

There was a law that prevented either horses or dogs, in particular trail dogs such as the limer, to be sold across the Border. Highly prized and fetching a fine price the borderers on both sides did what they did best, and ignored the law, even if the ultimate penalty was death. The dogs often changed hands for more than the other prized animal in the borders, the Galloway nag.

Truce Days

The Lochmaben or Clochmaben stone, near the shores of the Solway Firth on the Scottish side and Close to Gretna. This was a noted Truce site.

Keeping law and order in the borders was indeed a thankless task, in the absence of courts as we know them, this work fell to the wardens. When these crimes and misdemeanours happened across the Border this made the wardens' job even more difficult. To do this and settle other cross-Border matters the wardens held meetings. These meetings became events in themselves known as "days of truce".

The date of the day would be known far in advance and invitations to the hedesmen of each important family and the main earls and lords in order that they would attend. Summons would also be sent out by the wardens to those implicated in the bills so that they would appear. Proclamations about the day would be read out in the surrounding towns, informing all about the coming event.

Truce days lasted from sunrise on the day until sunrise on the next day. All people were given safe passage on these days. The thought of someone being free from apprehension on a truce day in the main was upheld, however probably the most notable breach of this rule of free passage was the capture of Kinmont Willie Armstrong by an English party in April 1596. This caused consternation in the borders and an Anglo-Scottish diplomatic storm.

They were days when a bill of complaint would be settled, often with noted reivers being listed as both the wronged and the wrongdoer.

Each pair of marches would hold their own days of truce, so the places where this happened would be a convenient place to both wardens. This meant that favoured places featured more than others, places like Kershopefoot, the Redeswire and the Lochmaben Stone on the Solway Firth. The days were popular with locals and stalls were set up on both sides, with pedlars and hawkers selling their wares.

The ritual on the day would be that the wardens from each side would approach each other until within hailing distance. The English warden would then hail the Scottish warden. A party from the English side would then ride towards the Scottish side to ask for assurance. When this was granted both parties would move forward to the meeting place for the meeting to commence, the meeting often lasting until sundown on the allotted day.

The bills for the day would be read out, a jury much like today would be selected. The English warden would pick six Scotsmen and the Scottish warden would pick six Englishmen to sit and hear the bills. The Scottish would hear the bills against English reivers and the English would hear the bills against Scottish reivers. These jurors would then be sworn in by the wardens. They were supposed to be good and just men with no thieves, thugs or murderers in the selection of the chosen men. How they ever managed to do this in the reiving times is a mystery as many of the claimants also had bills against them.

At the end of the day the findings would be read out like the starting proclamation but with the findings of the day. It would then be left to the wardens to collect the fines of those found guilty of crime. In the cases where the defendant was found guilty and sentenced to death, the wardens had such power invested in them. The condemned person would be taken away to be hung from a nearby tree or drowned in the river in what were known as murder holes.

Although the truce days were supposed to happen once a month, this was rarely the case. A variety of reasons prevented the meetings, sometimes it was that England and Scotland were at war, sometimes other business took precedence and then there was the fact that some wardens just did not get on or the wardens didn't like doing the truce days so they made up excuses so that the day didn't take place.

Whilst the truce days were supposed to be trouble free, this was not often the case as in the case of the Raid of the Redeswire on 7 July 1575 where a disagreement between the wardens, Sir John Carmichael on the Scottish side and Sir John Forster on the English side, escalated into a pitched battle.

The days of truce were disbanded after the Union of the Crowns in 1603 as the necessity for them ceased to exist.

The Wardens

The wardenry of the marches could be a candidate for the worst job in the world for the gentry of the sixteenth century. On both sides of the Border the wardens were appointed by the Crown. With the Border on each side being divided into three areas called marches, each march needed a warden and deputy warden, responsible for keeping law and order within their own march. These wardens had almost free rein to do as they pleased, they were the law in their own area. They also had to patrol the Border to stop raids from the other side of the Border and from within their own and the neighbouring marches.

The wardens were in a difficult position as the local farmers probably thought they didn't do enough to stop the raids. Most wardens tried their best to do the job, but on both sides the common complaint was money; to be more specific, not enough of it, either to do the job or for resources to do the job. Queen Elizabeth on the English side was noted for being stingy with the royal coffers as many a warden would testify and indeed did in writing to those in government at the time.

On the Scottish side the wardens came from the local gentry within that march. In the Scottish West March it tended to be the Maxwells or the Johnstones, in the early days the Douglases also held this position. In the Scottish Middle March it tended to be the Kerrs, either from Ferniehirst or Cessford. The wardens of the Scottish East March tended to be the sole preserve of the Humes (often spelt and pronounced Home) indeed they thought it theirs by right and when a Frenchman was appointed to the post, they duly ambushed him and despatched him to meet his maker rather earlier than he probably expected.

On the English side of the border the wardens, as a rule, were from the south and not from the locality. However there were exceptions, like Sir John Forster who held various positions in the east and middle marches. There were others who, like Sir Robert Carey, whilst not a Borderer had extensive knowledge of the borders due to the fact that his father Lord Hunsdon had served as East March warden and he had spent time there with his father. Other than the money, the main complaint from the wardens who were sent north was the cold, the biting north wind was not to their liking. One notable one for complaining about the cold was Peregrine Bertie, the 13th Baron Willoughby de Eresby who complained long and hard while the Governor of Berwick and Warden of the East March from 1598. He had replaced Sir Robert Carey in 1598 when Carey had gone back to the court of Queen Elizabeth, so it is with some irony that he died of a heavy cold in Berwick in 1601. He was buried in Lincolnshire, where in death he might not have been as cold as he was in Berwick.

The reason behind the use of outsiders for the position of warden of a march was that they were not so inclined to get tied into local family politics, feuds and general corruption as someone who was from the local area. It wasn't unknown on the English side for both father and son to serve as wardens. In the West March the Scropes of Bolton in Wenslydale served as warden with the younger Thomas Scrope following his father in the post. In the east March the Carey family provided three members, all eventually serving as wardens of the March. Lord Hunsdon also served as Lord Warden of the marches and his sons, Sir John Carey and Sir Robert Carey, both became wardens or deputy wardens.

On the English East March the wardenry was controlled from Berwick Castle, although there were significant garrisons at both Norham and Wark to make these castles very prominent on the borders. Sadly, today Wark is just a mound whilst both Berwick and Norham are in ruins. The Middle March was controlled from the enclaves of Alnwick Abbey. The West March is controlled by the impressive Carlisle Castle, still standing today and used as a museum. It was in use long after the Union of the Crowns as home to the Border Regiment.

The Scottish West March would be controlled from the relevant castle that the current incumbent of the office owned. When the Maxwells held the position they would control the March from Caerlaverock, the Johnstones from Lochwood and the Douglases from Threave or Drumlanrig. In the Middle March the Kerrs would control from either Cessford or Ferniehirst. Within the Middle March was also Liddesdale which required its own warden, known as the Keeper of Liddesdale. The base for this was Hermitage Castle often called the Strength of Liddesdale. Sometimes the Middle March wardens also held the Liddesdale position and other notable gentry have held the position, and so it was in 1566 when James Hepburn the Earl of Bothwell held the position and had to retake the Castle after an altercation with Little Jock Elliot when the Elliots overran Hermitage. In the east the Humes would control the March from either Hume Castle or Fast Castle.

The warden had to organise and lead a warden rode in order to reclaim goods taken by the reivers. He would also organise the days of truce with his opposite warden.

On the English side the wardens had to organise and oversee a muster of the men in their march to see what weaponry was available. From pitchfork and billhooks to muskets and to find out who was fit for service either in times of war, or for the rodes and trod. The information obtained from these musters was sent to London where it was recorded for the Crown. These musters could be done by village or by parish depending upon the geographical area.

When the Union of the Crowns came about in 1603, King James abolished the position of Warden of the March. The Border became what he referred to as his Middle Shires.

Food for Thought

A Black Galloway cow, native to the borders. The more famous belted was a later cross with a Dutch breed.

You would have thought that with all the raiding of cattle that the people of the borders and the reivers only ever ate prime beef. Whilst the wealthier families certainly had their fair share of the beef and the pickings, the cattle weren't the same as the well cultivated breeds we have today. The cattle were dual purpose in that not only did they provide the beef for the table, they also provided the milk, and when their life had finished the skins provided the leather for shoes and clothes. Most would probably be descended from the Black Galloway cattle we see today, only they would have been much thinner. These are native to the borders and have a thick coat to be able to survive the climate. Though Chillingham had its own breed of white cattle, these were less numerous and were contained within a walled park near the castle.

The sheep too had to provide both mutton and wool, they also needed to be hardy as they stayed out in the open moorland and were often the only animal that would survive. The Cheviot sheep is descended from those who would have roamed the border hills four hundred years ago. Pigs were kept in smaller numbers and mainly close to the homestead, whilst those taken during raids were not favoured as they travelled much more slowly than sheep or cattle. What was kept, in large numbers, for its milk, meat and skin were goats, as they would eat anything and needed little tending as they foraged for themselves. From the milk of both the goats and the cattle they would have made a crude type of cheese, which would have been eaten almost as soon as it was ready.

In most households across the Border, even the poorer ones, a pot of potage would be kept boiling on the fire. This stew-like substance would boil for hours and be kept hot by the fire. Into it would be put almost anything that was edible from parts of the animals or fish to root vegetables. Anything that was remotely nutritious would be put into the pot together with some water, although I have to say the goodness was probably boiled out of the ingredients given the length of time it was cooked.

When some excavations were done at Smailholm Tower near Kelso in the 1990s they found evidence of marine fish. This would mean that they would have brought the fish by horse and cart from either Berwick or Eyemouth for consumption. All types of fish would have been eaten, none would have been wasted, and we eat fewer types of freshwater fish today than in medieval times. For that reason the Tweed and its tributaries like the Till would have been a major source of food. Indeed the fish garth on the River Esk in Cumbria was hotly contested and controlled with a rod of iron by the Grahams.

Wild food wasn't wasted either, as most types of bird were killed and eaten, even starlings. Another favourite was squirrel or hedgehog, these would be rolled in earth or clay and then put on the fire which was like baking them in an oven. Deer were hunted, even by the poor; they could have been hung for stealing them if they had been caught.

Bread was eaten rarely as this often required an oven which most homes didn't have. There was also the scarcity of crops to make the bread from, as the population was quite fluid due to the constant raiding. Instead the oats would be done on a griddle to make a biscuit-like cake which would be eaten dry, much the same as a modern-day oatcake only with a rougher texture.

The main drink would have been beer. Different strengths of ale were produced and drank at different times of day, in the morning with breakfast a light beer with a low alcohol content would have been drunk. Later in the day and the evening a heavier beer would have been consumed. One of the main reasons for drinking beer all the time is that, in the brewing process, the water was boiled so it was safer to drink. It is interesting to note also that there are very few listings of borderers being drunk in the court papers.

Wine was made, often from the local summer fruits and only the rich and connected would get the imported wine. The fruit juice was also kept to drink at mealtimes. However the preservation of food and drink was primitive and it often only amounted to the salting of the meat.

Dressing the Part

When people think of the Tudor and later Elizabethan periods, they think of rich costumes, ruffs and fine tapestries. This may have been true at the royal court and high merchants but this couldn't be further from the truth in the borders, where basic functionality and survival were the order of the day.

The head would be covered with a cap or bonnet, underneath would often be worn a steel pot helmet, this was a basic round skullcap-type helmet with no frills, that gave the nickname to the Reivers in "the Steel Bonnets". Other helmets that were worn were the morion, much favoured on the continent and by Hollywood in their portrayal of this period. The morion was worn from the mid-sixteenth century through to the mid-seventeenth century, and had a comb on the top which, depending upon the size of the comb, denoted the rank of the person wearing the helmet: the higher the comb the higher the rank. After the morion, the burgonet was the favoured helmet, for like the morion it had a comb and was much favoured on the Continent, in earlier centuries the burgonet came with a more traditional face covering making a full helmet. These helmets were expensive to make and so were often worn by the wealthier reivers.

High comb Morian helmet favoured by Reivers.

After the helmet the reiver needed to be protected on his body. This was done by a sleeveless jacket or waistcoat called "a jack of plaite", often known just as a "jack". This was quilted with either metal, generally iron or bone, sewn into the quilting. This gave both lightness and strength against sword blows. The jack gave the wearer freedom of movement, in particular when he was mounted, allowing him to still use a sword or bow whilst in the saddle. The jack would extend to thigh-length so that it would give some protection to the upper thigh. The lower part of the thigh would be protected by stout thigh length riding boots. These would protect the lower leg too mainly from the elements.

Under the jack would be a doublet or coarse linen shirt depending upon how affluent the wearer was. When not out on a raid, the doublet would be covered by a leather waistcoat or jacket.

Armed and Dangerous

In a time when priests carried arms for self-protection and the locals really didn't need any excuse for a fight, it's no surprise to find the amount and diversification of arms that were used by the reivers.

A 16th century Ballack or Bollock dagger.

No self-respecting reiver would be without his ballock (bollock) dagger, probably the main weapon in the borders. About twelve inches long with two oval lumps at the base of the handle that resembled the male genitalia, hence the more common name of Bollock dagger. This weapon probably gave rise to the saying "to get a bollocking" in reference to being chastised or attacked with the weapon. The blade is usually double edged and around eight inches long.

An early 17th century basket hilted sword

The sword of choice on both sides of the Border was the basket-hilted broadsword, named due to the woven basket-type protection for the hand and that the blade was broader than the rapier or foil. These swords, on the border, were generally single edged with a thicker blunt back edge. Later the basket-type protection got more elaborate and decorative, but its primary task was still to protect the hand of the user. Blade length was generally about thirty inches from the handle to the tip of the blade. The blade would be kept well-oiled to make sure it could be drawn quickly from its leather scabbard.

To go with the sword and dagger the reiver might also carry a smaller parrying dagger. This would be used in the left hand of a right-handed person and used to parry or fend the blows of the opponent. These daggers incorporated a wider guard than a conventional dagger. Instead of the parrying dagger in Scotland, they would use a small shield called a buckler. This would also be used to parry or block the blows of an opponent, the buckler being between eight and eighteen inches in diameter.

The weapon that the reivers were the most famous for and that was used to great effect in wartime as well as in what could loosely be described as peacetime in the borders, was the lance or "lang spear" as it was often known. About eight feet in length with a pointed metal tip, it was a formidable weapon whether herding cattle to drive them over the Border, or spearing the opponent in a battle. So renowned were they for the use of this weapon that they were considered some of the finest light cavalry anywhere in Europe and a formidable opponent.

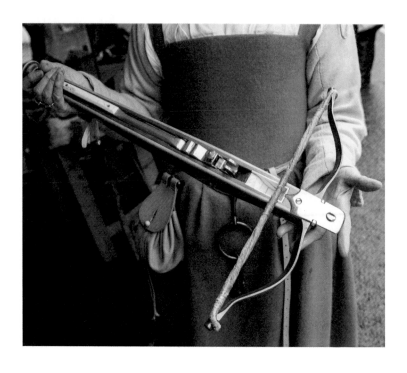

The Latch or small crossbow

In Scotland some reivers carried a small crossbow known as a latch; this would be worn on the belt. The weapon would be used like a small pistol, in the latter part of the sixteenth century. The English reivers at the same time preferred the English longbow.

Another particularly Scottish weapon or more interestingly one from the Jedburgh area of the borders was the Jeddart staff or axe. Calling this weapon an axe was in all probability wrong in that it was a six-oot long pole with a long blade at one end, a bit like a sword blade, mounted on the side of a pole. It is said that the smiths in Jedburgh had found a use for old sword blades, whether this is true or not there is no evidence, or whether the weapon was originally a farming implement used as a weapon in times of need.

As the sixteenth century progressed, firearms became more used and widely available, this started with matchlock rifles and progressed to the flintlock and to wheel-lock-triggered firearms. These included small pistols called daggs which were often carried in pairs. The biggest problem with the early firearms was the reload time which was considerably less than an English archer could discharge or loose his longbow. Accuracy in the early firearms was also a problem, without the later rifled barrels they were both notoriously inaccurate and unreliable.

Whatever way the reiver was armed, and they were heavily armed at times, on their horses they were some of the finest but probably the worst disciplined light cavalry the world has seen.

Passing the Time

The reiving season ran from Lammastide (1 August) to Candlemas (2 February), although raids did go on all year round. However what did they fill their time with when not out reiving someone else's goods?

The Fell Pony, shown with a handler, shares its DNA with the now extinct Galloway Nag of the Reiving times.

Horses played a big part in the lives of the people on the border, known as nags, Galloway nags, hobbys, or hobblers. Standing about fourteen hands high and very sure footed, they led their masters through some of the worst bogs and mosses in the borders. However, never shy of wanting a good horse, they also raced them, with the race meetings a common event and also a place to meet and do business. By business they would mean horse trading, even though at times trading horses and dogs across border was illegal and punishable by death, it happened frequently. The meetings also meant gambling, whether it was betting on the horse racing or playing cards and dice on the side. The race meeting could also be a place for plotting raids; the rescue of Kinmont Willie from Carlisle Castle was planned at a race meeting at Langholm.

Football was one of the main sports in the borders, played and loved as today on both sides. Played by all levels of the community, James Hepburn, Earl of Bothwell was by all accounts a mean player; so was Sir Robert Carey it probably goes without saying that the Charltons, Milburns and Robsons played. The game of football wasn't the sophisticated game that we see played today, some have likened it to rugby with few rules. It was more like a game called murder ball, which was still played in some Border schools in modern times, which is played like football with physical violence being encouraged rather than just permitted.

One of the earliest recorded games of football was arranged between the Armstrongs of Liddesdale and the garrison of Bewcastle. It was the captain of Bewcastle who arranged the match, although the date and the venue of this match is not recorded. What is recorded is that one of the local dignitaries at Bewcastle thought the match against the noted Armstrong reivers was not to be encouraged and that they should be arrested. So the dignitary, one Mr William Ridley, set an ambush for the Armstrongs together with some of his friends. Word of this got to the Armstrongs warning them of the ambush on the way from the match. Not short of local support the Armstrongs brought some two hundred followers to the game and turned the table on Ridley and his supporters. In the end two dead were left for dead and another whose bowels fell out, but were sewn back in. Unfortunately no one kept the actual score of the game.

In another border match one of the competitors was heard to shout "Never mind the ball, get on with the game!" Obviously at that time football didn't necessarily have the importance of the ball. It was also said that the good people of Jedburgh played football with the heads of captured English soldiers. How true this is I'm not sure but it is believable.

The numbers on each side were also the subject of some debate and not necessarily even, as no fixed rules existed to limit the sides, a game could have some two hundred competitors. Today in Jedburgh they have what is known as "Hand Ba" or "Jedhart Ba" which is played on the Thursday after Shrove Tuesday on what would have been known as Candlemas. It is a throwback to the game of football played during the Tudor period. In that two mob teams play for a ball and anything goes. The teams are the Uppies and the Doonies; the game starts at midday and lasts until the last ball is thrown with goals at both ends of the town. The ball or balls used today are smaller than used in a game of modern football.

A slightly more updated game is played in Alnwick each year on Shrove Tuesday. This Game is started by the Duke of Northumberland throwing a ball into the crowd assembled outside Alnwick Castle. There is the procession to the field called "The Pastures" where the pitch is about two hundred yards long. The game was moved to this field during the nineteenth century after locals complained about the game being played through the streets of Alnwick.

One of the biggest legacies that the border reivers have left us is in the poetry and the ballads of the history of the borders. These ballads were used to celebrate events and characters of the borders. It also tells us much of the history of the borders in the words of the borderers. During the reiving period the vast majority of the population was illiterate, only the monks and gentry could actually write, so the ballads were initially passed down by word of mouth. It was only when Sir Walter Scott produced his Minstrelsey of the Scottish Borders did the ballads get written down. Scott has been heavily criticised for this and for romanticising the reivers, but without his work and the publicity he gave to the area little would have been known. He also blended the tales into his own novels, further romanticising the reivers. The ballads in the borders continue to this day, Scott knew James Hogg (the Ettrick Shepherd) who wrote the poem *Lock the Door Larriston*. Later at the turn of the twentieth century W.H. Ogilvy wrote *The Wonderful Raiders* about a raid in the middle marches. This wonderful poem has been set to music by the Hawick band Scocha bringing the tradition up to the present day.

When we look at the original ballads we can see that a number of them run to a considerable number of verses, the *Ballad of Chevy Chase* or *The Battle of Otterburn* runs to some fifty-two verses, in some versions and only thirty-five in others and takes some time to read. Whichever way you wish to view the ballads and the poetry, it leaves us with an interesting mix of a breed of people who could murder one other in the blink of an eye and, in the next, leave you with some rich poetry.

Brinkburn Priory

Situated on a bend in the River Coquet, about four and a half miles south-east of Rothbury, this small priory was founded in 1135 in the reign of Henry I as part of the Augustinian order. The founder of the house was William Bertram of Mitford and he was its first prior. In the early years Brinkburn was a daughter – or sub-house of St Mary de Insula of Pentlney Norfolk and depended heavily upon its mother house for support. Little or nothing is known about the early history of the Priory as few documents exist; what does exist are housed in the British Museum. In 1180 the Priory became an independent house, at about the same time that the building of the church commenced. The charter for Brinkburn's status was confirmed in 1200 by King John, and reaffirmed later by Henry III in 1252.

Being near to the Scottish Border and to the reivers of Tynedale and Redesdale the Priory was open to attack and indeed it is recorded that in 1291 the house was attacked and again in 1331, 1333 and 1334. In 1419 the Priory was attacked again and burnt, however the church was still able to hold services.

It was never known as one of the wealthier priories, but nevertheless acquired lands in both Durham and Northumberland; indeed in 1391 the Priory was pleading poverty. When Henry VIII passed the act to dissolve the monasteries, which decreed that all monasteries having an annual income under £200 would be closed, Brinkburn fitted into this category as it had been recorded in the "valor Ecclesiasticus" that its annual income was a mere £69 in 1535, the year of the act. After the dissolution the lands at Brinkburn passed to the Fenwick family.

The Fenwick family later built the manor house on the site but retained the church. This they kept in good order until the end of the sixteenth century. Just prior to the union of the crowns, the church was reported to be in a state of disrepair and it was abandoned before the end of the seventeenth century when the roof collapsed.

In the early part of the nineteenth century, the manor house and the church were significantly restored. The church still retains some of its wonderful twelfth-century character.

Today there is only a faint trace of the early monastic settlement on the site. However, the manor house and church are in the care of English Heritage, accessible to all.

Dryburgh Abbey

Dryburgh Abbey is situated just north of the village of St Boswells at the start of St Cuthbert's way and on a bend in the River Tweed. It is the burial place for Sir Walter Scott and Field Marshall Earl Haig. Founded on 10 November 1150 by Hugh de Morville with canons from Alnwick Abbey in Northumberland, Dryburgh would be a daughter house to Alnwick Abbey. The founding canons brought with them in December 1152 canon Roger who would become the first abbot of the Abbey. The de Morville family had arrived in Scotland from Normandy at the time of William the Conqueror and settled near to Melrose, they were a major landowner in the area and Hugh de Morville was friends with David I of Scotland.

Like all Border Abbeys the position of Dryburgh meant it was under threat of attack from the English side, so it was in 1322 that Edward II's army burned the Abbey on their retreat from Scotland. In all likelihood the burnt Abbey would have been constructed from wood collected locally. What was rebuilt after the fire was the basis of the Abbey we see in ruins today. The Abbey was added to over the next century, yet it was sacked again in 1385 by another English army. The Abbey was again rebuilt and would see nearly another 150 years of use.

The Abbey was never as rich as nearby Melrose nor did it have Melrose's royal patronage. It owed much to the patronage of Hugh de Morville and his wife Beatrice de Beauchamp. However the original timber to build the Abbey came from the royal forest and was sanctioned by David I, who we presume must have been sympathetic to the construction of the Abbey by Hugh. Hugh entered the Abbey as a canon in 1162 leaving the Scottish family estates to his oldest son Richard. His youngest son, Hugh received the family lands in England.

The sad end as a monastery came on 4 November 1544 when English troops mounted a raid during the period known as "the Rough Wooing". The Abbey didn't get another reprieve as the Reformation in Scotland came in 1560 before it could be rebuilt again. After the Reformation James VI gave the Abbey and its lands to the Earl of Mar.

In 1786 the 12th Earl of Buchan bought the land and the Abbey, whereas today it is in the care of Historic Scotland and is open to all to visit. It is a majestic ruin and shows probably better than most the living quarters of the canons who inhabited the monastery over 500 years ago.

Hexham Abbey

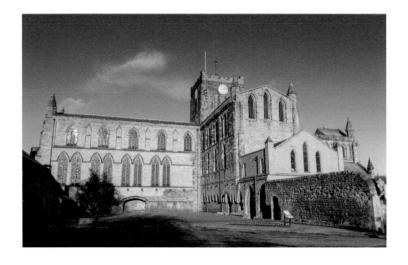

It is truly amazing that not only has this wonderful Abbey survived intact since the Reformation, but also that it continues to serve the town as its parish church. The history of the Abbey and the town are interlinked. A church has stood on the present site for over 1300 years and in all probability a place of worship has graced the site since the seventh century.

Etheldreda, Queen of Northumbria granted the lands around Hexham to Wilfred Bishop of York in around 674. The first abbey buildings were constructed from local wood and stone transported from the nearby Roman Wall and other ruins. This was populated with Benedictine monks. However in 875 the church was burnt down, when Halfdane the Dane pillaged Tynedale in a raid.

The Abbey passed to the control of the See of Durham at the beginning of the eleventh century. Eilaf of Durham controlled Hexham in 1050 and instructed the rebuilding of the church. He did not live to see the completion and this was done by his son,

Eilaf II. The greater part of the present church dates from around this time, although the earliest part is the crypt which dates to Saxon times.

With its proximity to the Scottish Border, Hexham wasn't spared Scottish raids. In 1346 a retreating army under David II sacked the Abbey and burnt it whilst retreating from the Battle of Neville's Cross.

In 1514 the Bishop of Hexham participated in a raid into Scotland, resting just south of Hawick in a place known as Hornshole. The party were surprised and the Bishop's banner taken by the young callants[2] of Hawick. A replica of the banner was lent to the town by Hawick in 1914 to commemorate the 400th anniversary of the battle.

Hexham like other religious places suffered under the Dissolution of the monasteries in 1536. In 1537 the canons were pensioned off and Henry VIII gifted the lands of the Abbey to Sir Reynold Carnaby. The dormitory was then disused and soon fell into disrepair, completely crumbling in the next century.

After the Abbey had been disbanded in 1537 the windows were destroyed. These were repaired in 1873 under the patronage of Bentham and Eleanor Hall, to show the beautiful windows we see today.

Today the Abbey is in the diocese of Newcastle and still operates as a parish church, with Sunday and weekly services throughout the year. It is open all year for the public to visit.

---

[2] Callants are the young men of the town

Jedburgh Abbey

Situated on the south side of Jedburgh town and close to the Jed water are the ruins of Jedburgh Abbey, where there has been a church on the site since the eighth century. Originally Jedburgh was part of the Kingdom of Northumbria and administered from its capital at Bamburgh. The town was part of the See of Lindisfarne, at this time it was only a small church.

In 1118 before he became King of Scotland, David founded a monastery at Jedburgh, with Augustinian canons from Saint-Quentin at Beauvais in France. The Priory was in existence in 1139 and run by a prior named Daniel. It received priory status later in David's reign and then, just before his death, it was given full monastery status and was dedicated to the Virgin Mary.

When David died, as his son Henry had predeceased him, the patronage of the Abbey passed to his grandsons Malcolm IV (known as Malcolm the Maiden), and was succeeded by William I often called William the Lion, his other grandson. Malcolm died at Jedburgh in 1165. As the Kingdom of Northumbria rescinded the town of Jedburgh and its Abbey became a major point on the journey across the Scottish Border from England.

At the end of the thirteenth century Alexander III married his young bride Yolande de Dreux at Jedburgh in 1285, by which time the nave and choir placing were complete. The death of Alexander in 1286 was the beginning of the Scottish wars of independence. The Abbot of Jedburgh swore fealty to Edward I in 1296, probably to keep the large lands the Abbey had acquired in Northumberland. Like the other border abbeys, Jedburgh was exposed to English raiding as armies regularly crossed the Border. It was wrecked and pillaged in 1297 after the Earl of Surrey's defeat at the battle of Stirling Bridge.

The patronage of the Abbey at this time had passed to Robert I "the Bruce"; he carried this patronage until his death in 1329. The Abbey was again sacked in 1346 after the Scottish defeat at Neville's Cross. The Abbey was rebuilt and indeed David II instigated the building of the north transept in 1370, which is still in evidence today.

The Abbey faced more destruction during the Wars of the Roses in the fifteenth century. This indeed was a precursor to the destruction wreaked in 1523 by Earl of Surrey and in 1544 by the Earl of Hertford during the "Rough Wooing". The end for the Abbey came with the reformation in 1560; it ceased to function as a religious order.

The Abbey continued to be used as a parish church until around 1671. In 1871 the ruins of the church were declared unsafe and all worship was stopped. The Abbey and church were given to the state in 1917, so today the ruins are in the careful hands of Historic Scotland.

Kelso Abbey

The Abbey at Kelso is different to other border abbeys and priories with the exception of Hexham in that it is in the middle of the town and not on the outskirts or positioned remotely. But like others it is in close proximity to a river, being at the confluence of the River Tweed and River Teviot. The Abbey not only served the town of Kelso, but in earlier times the royal town of Roxburgh.

The Abbey was founded at the request of David I in the twelfth century by Tironensian monks, a reformed Benedictine order. The monks had come to Selkirk Abbey from Tiron in France in 1113, when David had control of southern Scotland and the establishment of the royal burgh at Roxburgh which would have been what we would regard as a new town. Under the guidance of the Bishop of Glasgow, David moved the monks from Selkirk to Kelso in 1128 and founded the Abbey there. The actual construction of what we see today is believed to have started in 1143.

With its position in sight of the royal castle at Roxburgh and its royal patronage, the abbey became one of the wealthiest in Scotland. It would, in all probability, have a large part to play in the significant wool trade in the area and its position at the west end of the very fertile area known as "the Merse" would have helped it. The drawback to this is the close proximity to the English Border, however.

In 1460 the young King James III was crowned in the Abbey after his father James II was killed by an exploding canon whilst besieging the English held Roxburgh Castle. During the sixteenth century the Abbey was the subject of numerous English attacks. With Henry VIII conducting the war of the Rough Wooing and then the Earl of Hertford continuing the attacks after Henry's death in 1547, Kelso sustained major damage during this period.

With the Reformation in 1560 there were fewer monks at Kelso, although a small number continued until the Abbey was finally closed, as a religious order, in 1587. The Abbey lands passed to the Kers of Cessford in 1607. During the sixteenth century while the parish church was still used, the other buildings were relieved of their stone for new buildings in the town. At the start of the nineteenth century large parts of the site were cleared, leaving what we see today.

Today the Abbey is under the care of Scottish Heritage and is accessible to the public.

Lanercost Priory

Never has a priory been so linked with the sword and the cross as Lanercost, a favourite staying place of Edward I on his way north in his attempts to subdue Scotland. He spent five months at the Priory in 1306-7 before moving on to Burgh by Sands and his death there in 1307. It is also linked to the Dacre family of nearby Naworth Castle, indeed Sir Thomas Dacre is buried in the Priory.

The Augustinian Priory of Lanercost with its little church of St Mary Magdalene lies just south of Hadrian's Wall in north Cumbria. Stone from the Wall was most probably used to build parts of the Priory, as Roman inscriptions have been found in the walls. Robert de Vaux dedicated the land to the canons in about 1170. Unlike other priories, which were originally built of wood, it appears that from the start Lanercost was built at least in part from stone, with the bulk of the buildings dating from the thirteenth century.

Being on the Border the Priory, which received its tithes from the surrounding area, suffered with, not only, the strain of a royal visit but the ensuing Border wars. This led to the funds of the

Priory being depleted. Edward I wasn't the only royal to stay at Lanercost, Robert the Bruce stayed for three days in 1311, although it is thought that his stay was not as welcome as that of Edward's, as Robert imprisoned some of the canons when he visited. They were however later freed, with a truce and agreement between Robert and Edward III in 1328, bringing some respite and with it a cordial relationship between Lanercost and Kelso Abbey.

Henry VIII the scourge of the monasteries closed Lanercost in 1538; the lands were passed to the Dacre family on the dissolution and then through marriage to the Howards. The church however continued to be used as the local parish church. This was redecorated in the seventeenth century. The nave was re-roofed in 1747, but the Priory was on its way to ruin, with the roof collapsing around the middle of the nineteenth century. The Howards put the ruins into public hands in 1929; today it is owned and ministered by English Heritage.

Lindisfarne Priory

Nestled on a flat area of the small island of Lindisfarne (also known as Holy Island), and situated off the northern Northumberland coast, this wonderful Priory could be said to be the cradle of Christianity in England. Next to a natural harbour and today watched over by the small castle on the rock, it makes an idyllic scene.

The Irish monk St Aiden settled here with his Celtic brethren in around 634. These were Celtic monks and wore their hair shaved back at the front and long at the back, unlike the Roman monks who wore the tonsure. This may also explain why the freshwater lake on the Island is called the Lough with the Irish spelling and not either lake or the Scottish loch which would have been more likely. Aiden and his monks came from the remote island monastery of Iona on the west coast of Scotland; this was at the request of King Oswald of Northumbria. The Kingdom of Northumbria at the time of Oswald and Aiden stretched from the Humber in the south to the Forth in the north. Oswald himself was brought up at the royal house situated at Dunadd Fort, the capital of Dal Riada, a kingdom to the West of Scotland that also stretched into Northern Ireland.

The buildings in the seventh century would have been small and functional and not the grand ruins that we see today. Aiden became the first bishop of Northumbria, with the gift of the land on Lindisfarne in sight of Oswald's castle at Bamburgh ten kilometres to the south and within reach of his great hall at Yeavering, near Wooler. Aiden remained at Lindisfarne and administered to the local population on the mainland, all the while retaining links to the mother house on Iona. This carried on with the next two bishops Finan, who built a wooden church, and Colman. In 664 the synod at Whitby decided to follow the Roman method of calculating Easter, at that time the most important date in the Christian calendar. Some of the monks at Lindisfarne left at this time returning to the mother house of Iona, the ones that were left followed the new date and the Roman Catholic ways.

St Cuthbert arrived at Lindisfarne in around 670 after having been at Melrose Abbey. Cuthbert did more to align the Priory with the Roman Catholic ways, before deciding to become a hermit on the Farne Islands; he was recalled from this in 685 to be made, firstly, Bishop of Hexham and then Bishop of Lindisfarne. This however lasted only two years with Cuthbert again withdrawing to Inner Farne and dying there in 687.

In the late eighth century Lindisfarne together with most of Northumbria was raided by Vikings. With the raids becoming more frequent and violent during the early part of the ninth century, the monks decided to leave Lindisfarne in 875 taking the body of St Cuthbert with them, settling near to Chester le Street. They did briefly return to Lindisfarne complete with St Cuthbert's relics to evade the harrying of William the Conqueror and his troops, around 1070.

The monastery was refounded in 1069 with Benedictine monks, this time as a cell or outpost of Durham where St Cuthbert's remains were finally laid to rest. It would be around this time that the stone buildings would start to take shape. At this time in Lindisfarne's history it would be a peaceful, quiet existence for the monks. All that changed with the invasion of Scotland by Edward I in 1296, starting the first war of Scottish independence. Until then the Priory had patrons on both sides of the Border. With the war the tithes or fees that the Priory could collect from the locality were greatly reduced. Over the next 200 years the Priory was fortified and kept a small armoury.

The Priory was finally closed on the orders of Henry VIII in 1537, as Lindisfarne fell into the category of the poorer of the abbeys and priories which were closed first, as with an income of around £48 it fell well short of the minimum required of £200 to stay open. The building unlike others remained in the possession of the mother house at Durham as its income was substantially more.

The Priory finally fell into disrepair in the seventeenth century. Today it is in the hands of English Heritage for all to visit.

Melrose Abbey

Melrose Abbey is often referred to as "Fair Melrose" with its royal connections that go back to Scotland's King David I. Even today the ruins of this once glorious Abbey are magnificent, standing tall against the skyline you wonder how they built it without all the modern tools we have today.

The Cistercian monastery was founded in 1136 under the instruction of David I on the banks of the River Tweed. It was built on the site of an older monastery dedicated to St Aiden of Lindisfarne. The town of Melrose grew around the Abbey and as the Abbey grew so did the town as it gave the town shelter. Finally it was dedicated like all Cistercian monasteries to St Mary on 28 July 1146.

Due to the Border locality the Abbey suffered. In 1322 it was raided and heavily destroyed along with the town by Edward II, Robert the Bruce ordered its rebuilding. Bruce's heart is said to have been buried in the grounds of the Abbey church, after being taken on a crusade by Sir James Douglas, the Black Douglas, who acted as auditor for the rebuild that was undertaken by Robert the Bruce.

A heart in a lead casket was found during excavations in 1996 in the locality of the chapter house. This had been the second time it had been excavated, as earlier in the twentieth century the casket had been discovered and reburied.

The Abbey suffered again at the hands of the English when in 1385 the army of Richard II burned the Abbey, whilst battling with the Scottish army of Robert II. This time the rebuilding of the Abbey took nearly 100 years. James IV visited the Abbey in 1514 prior to the Battle of Flodden and parts were still unfinished. It is unclear whether or not he stayed at the Abbey.

The demise of Melrose sadly came in the sixteenth century, when in the war of the "Rough Wooing" the Abbey was badly damaged by Henry VIII's army. There didn't appear to be the will to repair the monastery this time and it ceased to be a working abbey. The last Abbot was the illegitimate son of James V, James Stuart who died in 1559, with the last monk finally dying in 1590.

Oliver Cromwell assaulted the Abbey during the Civil War leaving canon damage. The church had been converted and used as a parish church in 1610. In 1561 after the dissolution of the monasteries, the extensive Abbey lands which had been increased over the years by various Scottish monarchs enriching the Abbey were taken by the Crown. These lands were then split up and divided amongst local landowners. A significant portion of the lands along with the fishing rights to the River Tweed were conceded to the Scotts of Buccleuch by James VI.

The Abbey was built in a cross formation and even today its highest point, the principal tower, reaches a height of eighty-four feet. It has been painted by J M W Turner and mentioned in the Sir Walter Scott poem *The Lay of the Last Minstrel.* Melrose Abbey is in the care and trust of Historic Scotland and can be viewed by the public.

Sweetheart Abbey

Nestling near the River Nith and only eight miles from the town of Dumfries, are the impressive remains of the Cistercian Abbey of Sweetheart or New Abbey as it was known. The Abbey was founded in 1273 by Lady Devorguilla the wife of John Balliol and mother of the future King of Scotland, John Balliol.

Devorguilla founded the Abbey on the death of her husband, with monks from Dundrennan Abbey, which was the mother house of Sweetheart Abbey and why it was then called New Abbey. At his death Devorguilla had John's heart embalmed and placed in a silver and ivory casket. This was buried with her when she died in 1289, upon which the monks then called the Abbey Sweetheart in honour of Devorguilla. The elder John Balliol was himself a benefactor and also held considerable lands in England, most notably Barnard Castle; he also founded Balliol College in Oxford.

In its early days the monks of the Abbey played host to King Edward I of England in 1300, though he only stayed one night before moving on. The Abbey received a second patron in the late fourteenth century to help it, in the form of Archibald 'the Grim' Douglas, the Earl of Douglas, who gave generously to the abbey. Yet in 1397 the Abbey was hit by lightning and a fire ensued destroying large parts of it.

The Abbey is built from red sandstone that had been quarried locally and it is laid out in the form of a cross and is an impressive ruin. The full abbey grounds extend to thirty acres.

Unfortunately the end of Sweetheart as a monastery came, like so many religious establishments, after the Reformation in 1560. The downward spiral of the Abbey was slower than most, due to the patronage and protection of Lord Maxwell at Caerlaverock Castle, a noted Catholic. The last Abbot, Gilbert Brown continued practising the old religion after the Reformation, yet was imprisoned at Blackness Castle for this, However he was released and his belongings burnt in the street at Dumfries. The Abbott was exiled to France in 1608 where he died four years later.

Abbey buildings were slowly dismantled and the stone was used to build other dwellings locally. In 1779 the locals subscribed to preserve what was left of the buildings. Sir William Paterson, the founder of the Bank of England, was buried at Sweetheart Abbey in 1719. The Abbey and remainder of the grounds were handed over to the state in 1928, so today the Abbey is looked after by Historic Scotland.

Other Border Abbeys and Priories

Alnwick Abbey

All that is left of Alnwick Abbey is the fourteenth century gatehouse, situated in Hulne Park, a hunting park attached to Alnwick Castle. Founded in 1147 as a daughter house of Newhouse Abbey in Lincolnshire with Premonstratensian monks, during reiving times it was the base for the Warden of the English Middle March. Dissolved in 1535 and reformed a year later, it was dissolved for the last time in 1539.

Blanchland Abbey

Founded in 1165 as a daughter house of Croxton Abbey in Leicestershire with Premonstratensian monks, the abbot's house is now the Lord Crewe Hotel and dates from the fourteenth century in its earliest parts. The Abbey was pillaged and sacked during the Anglo-Scottish wars at regular intervals. The Abbey was dissolved in 1539, with the lands eventually passing into the hands of the Forster family. The local houses in the square were built from the stone of the Abbey. The church survives and is still in use, today.

Coldingham Priory

The Benedictine Priory was formed with monks from Durham in the reign of David I of Scotland who did much to found abbeys along Scotland's Border. It was constructed in 1100 and presented to David, yet the first Prior didn't take office here until 1147. Part of the Priory was destroyed by King John in 1216, after which the Priory was rebuilt larger that it had been previously. In 1509 the Priory severed all links with Durham to come under the control of Dunfermline Abbey. The English armies invading Scotland in 1537 and again in 1547 badly damaged this Priory. The church was restored in the 1660s and is still used as a parish church today.

Hulne Friary

Founded as a Carmelite Friary in 1240, the walls of this well-fortified monastery are still standing, along with its two-storey fifteenth-century gatehouse. It's situated about two miles from Alnwick Abbey gatehouse within Hulne Park. The Friary was dissolved in 1538 when a lot of the buildings were demolished.

Wetheral Priory

Situated on the outskirts of Carlisle, and like Alnwick only the gatehouse remains today of a once grand monastery. Founded in 1106 with Benedictine monks as a daughter house of St Mary's Abbey in York. The gatehouse was built in the fifteenth century, and would probably have had links to St Bees monastery which was also a daughter house of York. The Priory offered Edward II hospitality in 1301 and again in 1307 before he became king. Edward III offered those who sought sanctuary here a pardon in 1322 on provision they fought for him against the Scots. This Priory was finally dissolved in 1538.

The Battle of Ancrum Moor
27 January 1545

The battle site at Ancrum moor looking north from the Liliard stone.

Henry VIII of England had been desperate to marry his young son Edward to the daughter of James V of Scotland, the newly born Mary Queen of Scots. At first the Scots agreed to the union, however they changed their mind and offered the young Mary's hand to the King of France for his young son the Dauphin, this being readily agreed by both parties, further infuriating Henry.

In 1542 an English force had landed near Edinburgh and laid waste to the borders. James V had sent an army of nearly 20,000 Scots west, yet he split his forces and they were soundly defeated at the Battle of Solway Moss by a much smaller English force. This sent James into delirium and he died a few weeks later, leaving the infant Mary in the hands of a regent, the Earl of Arran. Henry saw this as a signal to pursue again the marriage of Edward to the infant Mary and began what became known as "the War of the Rough Wooing".

In 1544 English forces under the control of Sir Ralph Eure, at the time the Warden of the English Middle March, and Sir Brian Layton the Governor of Norham Castle, laid waste to the Scottish side of the borders again. In a time where life was cheap and brutality the norm, Eure and Layton stand out as some of the most greedy and ruthless, even barbaric men of their time. King Henry had promised Eure all the lands he captured for himself. He followed this directive with gusto, burning and beating his way through the borders.

Eure and Layton had with them some 5,000 troops made up of about 3,000 Spanish and German mercenaries, 1,500 English border reivers. They also had about 500 Scottish border reivers, those that had sworn allegiance to Henry. Among reivers the family loyalty meant more than the loyalty to whichever crown they had been paid by.

Eure and Layton's force plundered Melrose and its abbey and then headed for the town of Jedburgh and the Abbey that lay within that town. In response to this the Earl of Angus gathered together a Scottish force and tracked the English without engaging them at first. In February 1545 the English camped on Ancrum Moor just north of Jedburgh. The Earl of Angus' force, now numbering about 1200 and ready to engage, were joined by Sir Norman Leslie the Master of Rothes who brought with him 1200 lancers. They were also joined by Scott of Buccleuch and his Scottish borderers.

The Scottish camped on Gersit Law. Once encamped a small number of Scots attacked the English lines in a feint; the English, thinking they were the main force, gave chase. Yet by then it was late afternoon and, with the sun setting in the west where the Scots were camped, the English had the sun in their eyes. As they came over the top of Palace Hill they found they had run directly into the main Scottish force and fell upon the Scottish lances. As the battle turned in favour of the Scots, the Scottish border reivers on the English side and indeed some of the English reivers, who no doubt were related to the Scots either directly or through marriage, tore off their English identification and joined the Scottish cause. After this the remnants of the English force had to scatter through the hostile Scottish border countryside and find their way home.

The Battle was a disaster for Henry and for England, losing 800 men including the leaders Eure and Layton. It is understood that the Scots lost less than ten men in the Battle. The Scottish Regent, the Earl of Arran visited the battlefield afterwards and was shown the bodies of Eure and Layton.

Whilst this effectively ended this part of the "War of Rough Wooing", the next part began after King Henry's death under the Earl of Hertford when he, as the Duke of Somerset, was made the Regent and Protector for the boy king, Edward VI.

The Liliard stone serves as a memorial to the battle, it is said that the fair maiden Liliard, having seen her lover slain by the English picked up his sword and waded into the English ranks during the battle, until she herself was cut down. She is said to be buried under the Liliard stone.

The Battle of Arkinholme
1 May 1455

Arkinholme today, in the border hills above the town of Langholm

Often known as the Battle of Langholm this is a decisive battle in a Scottish civil war within Scotland, between the crown held by James II and the Black Douglases of Dumfries and Galloway. Though only a relatively small action with only a few hundred troops on either side it nevertheless resulted in a major power shift in the Scottish borders.

The fifteenth century in Scotland was a troublesome time. Insecure kings and warring lords and earls all led to turbulence with its belligerent and opportunist neighbours, England, always ready to take advantage. In the north-west and the Isles the McDonalds held sway, in the south-west the Black Douglases held the power. Although there were links between the Red Douglases of Angus and their border namesakes the Black Douglases, they were third cousins. The two branches of the family were never close. The 'red' and 'black' denoted their complexions rather than any other connotation that might have been thought of at the time.

William, the 8th Earl Douglas, being murdered by James II over dinner at Stirling Castle on 24 November 1440, his brother James took the title 9th Earl of Douglas and set about, in true border fashion, avenging his brother's death. The new Earl Douglas was supported by his younger twin Archibald Douglas, the Earl of Murray, their younger brother Hugh Douglas, Earl of Ormonde, and John Douglas, Lord of Balvenie. Howevera setback occurred when their ally James Hamiton, the 1st Lord Hamilton, defected from their cause.

James Douglas the 9th Earl sought help for his cause from Henry VI, as the English court had been willing to fan the flames of unrest in Scotland to further their own quest for the throne. As the Battle took place whilst the 9th Earl was seeking help, he did not participate in it; however the other three brothers all took part.

The royal army was being raised by George Douglas the 4th Earl of Angus, though there is some dispute as to whether he was at the Battle in person. The army consisted mainly of border families opposed to the Black Douglases, the Crichtons, the Maxwells, the Scots and the Johnstones, in fact some say that the Lord John Johnstone actually led the royal force.

Before the forces met at Arkinholme the Douglases had lost their castle at Abercorn near Linlithgow. Little is known about the actual Battle save for the fate of the Douglas brothers. Archibald Douglas was killed in battle, his head being planted on a spear and presented to King James. Hugh Douglas being captured and executed a short time later. John Douglas escaped and joined his brother the 9th Earl in England.

Shortly after the Battle the last of the Douglas castles, Threave in Dumfries and Galloway fell, bringing to a close the rule of the Black Douglases in the borders and their influence in Scotland. Later in the summer of 1455 the lands of the Douglases were attained and redistributed among other notable families, loyal to King James.

The Battle of Dryfe Sands
6 December 1593

Dryfe Sands today is peaceful farmland, a far cry from the battlefield of 1593.

In an age and an area littered with family feuds, where each family appeared to feud with all the others around it, none epitomised the feud or lasted longer than the one between the Maxwells and the Johnstones in the Scottish West March. The feud lasted for almost fifty years. In the latter part of the sixteenth century, culminating in the Battle of Dryfe Sands, although the actual feud didn't subside for another two generations.

Both the Maxwells and the Johnstones were prominent families in the Scottish West March. The Maxwells had their powerbase at Caerlaverlock Castle near Dumfries. The Johnstones power base being at Lockwood Tower, further to the north near what is now called Johnstonebridge. Both families had held the office of warden of the Scottish West March at various times during the fifteenth and sixteenth centuries. There is no doubt that the Maxwells were the more powerful of the families. However each families made it uncomfortable for the other when they held the wardenship.

Lochwood Tower, the home of the Johnstone family in 1593.

The feud started to come to a head in 1585 when the Maxwells burnt Lochwood Tower. Then, later in the same year, the Maxwells partly burned the town of Lockerbie, thus enraging the Johnstones. About this time they also captured Sir Johnnie Johnstone and imprisoned him harshly in Caerlaverlock Castle. Something Sir John never really recovered from, dying in 1587, he never gave up the feud until the end. The family baton then passed to his son James Johnstone, who in border fashion continued the feud.

There was an attempt to end the feud in 1592 with James Johnstone coming to an agreement with the Maxwells. Later in that year came two raids by the Johnstones on the Crichtons of Upper Nithsdale. The upshot of these raids was the hanging of William Johnstone of Wamphray and the widows of the Crichtons of Nithsdale taking the bloody shirts of the slain menfolk to Edinburgh and King James VI. The idea behind this would be to shame King James into action and reprisal against the Johnstones.

The Maxwells, who held the West March wardenship at the time, made an agreement with a number of other Nithsdale families, including the Grahams and Elliots from Liddesdale and the Crichtons from Sanquhar. Also included were the Irvines, Murrays, Carruthers and the Douglas' of Drumlanrig. In all an army close to 2,000 men who marched out of Dumfries in December, 1593.

The army sent a forward scouting party under the leadership of Captain Oliphant. The Johnstones were forewarned and James Johnstone raised a counter army to meet Maxwell. The Johnstones met the advanced party of Captain Oliphant and defeated them near Lochmaben, Oliphant was killed and the rest of the advance party fled and hid in the Lochmaben Kirk, as the church was called. The Johnstones promptly set fire to it, upon which the inhabitants surrendered.

The next day the main part of the Maxwell force set up position on the banks of the Dryfe Water near the town of Lockerbie. Johnstone held a position overlooking the Maxwell position. James Johnstone used a small party of horsemen to goad the Maxwells into attacking them, the horsemen then turned and fled with the Maxwells in hot pursuit, the main Johnstone army then fell upon the Maxwells sending panic throughout the ranks. From advanced positions the Maxwells fled back, straight into their own men. Some fled the battlefield as quickly as possible, Maxwell himself was killed in the battle. Legend has it that he was struck on the head by Lady Johnstone of Kirkton with the tower keys. His head was then severed and mounted on a lance by William Johnstone of Kirkton and taken back to Lochwood to claim the five-pound reward from James Johnstone.

In 1595 a force of Maxwells raided the Johnstone lands and captured a number of Johnstone family members. These were set free when a force of Johnstones drove the Maxwells out of Annandale. In true to Border life and showing how weak the King's position in this area actually was, further from being punished for the Battle, he was rewarded with the wardenry of the West March in 1596.

The feud didn't end with the Battle of Dryfe Sands, but continued with the new Lord Maxwell. A meeting was arranged in 1608 between Maxwell and James Johnstone to end the feud, the upshot of which was that Maxwell shot Johnstone in the back and then left Scotland. In his absence Maxwell was sentenced to death. When he returned to Scotland in 1612 Maxwell was handed over to the authorities by the Earl of Caithness and executed. This finally put an end to the longest running feud in the borders.

The area beside Dryfe Water said to be where Maxwells Thorn is located.

Battle of Flodden Field
9 September 1513

Flodden Field today, looking from the cross and the English position towards where the Scottish army was positioned.

On the 10 of September 1513 it was said a wail reverberated over the whole of Scotland. Scotland had suffered the greatest defeat ever at the hands of the Auld Enemy England on a lonely, remote Northumberland field. The Battle of Flodden Field had left Scotland bereft of its popular King James IV and most of its nobility. James became the last British monarch to die in battle.

The battle fought on Flodden Field near the tiny village of Branxton near Wooler is sometimes called the Battle of Branxton; however, the Battle of Flodden is by far its most common name.

Henry VIII was already embroiled in a war with France, when James IV declared war on England in support of France, in honour of the Auld Alliance. This had the effect of James being excommunicated, after sending ships to the aid of the French King Louis XII. In effect, this broke the peace treaties already in place with England on 28 June 1513. Subsequently, James wrote to Henry on 26 July 1513, whilst Henry was in France engaged in the siege of Therouanne, to ask if he would desist in attacking France as it was in breach of their treaty. Henry replied that James was mistaken and that any attempt to invade England would be resisted.

The Flodden Cross monument sitting on Flodden Hill.

James began the invasion of England in late August 1513 with an army of 30,000 men, having given England a month's notice of the invasion. James then moved to Ellenford, north of Duns, where he would join the Earl of Angus and the Earl of Home. They then crossed the River Tweed on the 24 August 1513 to hold a council of war.

After much disagreement between the commanders and James, the Scots moved south to attack, firstly, Norham castle, where there is some disagreement whether the great gun 'Mons Meg' was used. It is said that the Scots used Meg from the northern bank of the Tweed to fire balls eighteen inches in diameter at Norham until it finally surrendered on 29 August 1513. The Scots then moved to take Ford Castle on 1 September 1513. James left Ford Castle, burning it on the 4 September 1513, and camped on Flodden Hill.

Thomas Howard the Earl of Surrey heard of the Scottish invasion at Pontefract on 25 August 1513. The English army was raised and marched from York to Durham, and northward, camping overnight at Newcastle on 30 August 1513. They arrived at Alnwick on 3 September 1513 and provisioned a full complement of supplies to last until 9 September 1513.

Whilst the English army camped at Alnwick was taking on provisions, the Scottish army moved south in Northumberland to finally camp on Flodden Hill. On the 5 September 1513 Surrey sent an envoy to James with an offer of battle for the 9 September 1513 and no quarter. The envoy was captured by James but another was sent back to Surrey with the acceptance of battle. On the 6 September 1513 the English moved north to Wooler. The original envoy was released and returned to Surrey with news of the Scottish fortifications on Flodden Hill.

Surrey moved the English army north via Barmoor and Twizel to approach Branxton from the north. James then moved the Scottish army to defend Branxton Hill. Battle began late afternoon on 9 September, 1513.

Twizel Bridge over the River Till, opened in 1511 and used by both armies to move ordenance across the river.

At the start of the Battle the Scots had an estimated 30,000 pikemen trained by the French, the English about 10,000, mainly armed with billhooks, yet with a notable number of Archers. With both armies now in their formative positions, the Battle would commence with a volley from the Scottish cannons. The Scottish fired but the cannon fire went over the heads of the English. However, from their position the Scots didn't know the state of the boggy ground between them and the English army. Due to the rain earlier in the day, the dip between the two armies had become very boggy and this is where most of the Battle took place, in what became known as the killing field.

The Battle became three separate battles, a central area and two flanks on either side. The earls of Hume and Huntley with their Scottish borderers on the left flank moved to engage Edmund Howard on the English right flank. Howard and his men were overwhelmed by the Scottish forces. It was the arrival of Sir Christopher Dacre and his Prickers (light cavalry) that saved the day for the English right flank.

The Scottish army was armed with the long pike, favoured by the French. This proved ineffectual and cumbersome in the conditions that day on Flodden. The English were armed with the short and stout billhook and halberd, much more effective for close-quarter fighting.

Upon seeing the initial success of Hume and Huntley the central Scottish column advanced, only to get stuck in the mud low down in the dip between Flodden Hill and Branxton Hill: here they were cut down at close quarter by the English billhooks. Following the first wave of the Scots army, King James and his knights advanced towards the English lines but suffered the same fate: a fate compounded for them by the arrival on the English left flank of Stanley and his archers armed with the English longbow and sealed the King's fate. In just a few short hours the Scots had lost 10,000 men and the English 4,000. More importantly the Scots had lost their King James IV and an enormous amount of their nobility. No one in Scotland was left untouched by the Battle.

It has been said, without any substance, that the English played football with the heads of the dead Scots. A more interesting account is that Sir Christopher Dacre found and recognised the body of King James, who it is well known was friendly with King James because of his office as the warden of the English West March. He had played cards with the King and often taken the King's money from him in these games. He picked up the King's body wrapped him in his cloak and took it to the little church of Branxton, where he laid it near to the altar where it rested overnight before being taken back to Scotland.

Today Flodden is a peaceful place. A stone cross stands on the hill occupied by the English army, the tune *The Flowers of the Forest* remembers Scotland's dead.

The small chuch at Branxton, said to be where King James IV body lay the night after the battle.

The Battle of Halidon Hill
19 July 1333

Halidon Hill battle site today, on a hill north of Berwick upon Tweed.

Robert the Bruce in his deathbed declaration called "the Testament" said that the Scots should never fight the English in entrenched positions or pitched battle; instead they should fight a guerrilla-type war with a scorched-earth policy. In 1330 with the English military might in its ascendancy and the English use of the longbow at its most deadly, the English war machine struck terror though most of Europe.

How three years later the Scots at Halidon Hill near Berwick must have wished they had listened to the Testament.

In 1330 when Edward III came to the throne of England he had a claim to the throne of Scotland along with Edward Balliol, a cousin of the Bruce's. The town of Berwick-upon-Tweed at that time was held by the Scots. Even though the English-Scottish

Border had been defined in the Treaty of York in 1237, the two belligerents still fought over the town.

Balliol took a force north in 1330 and defeated a Scots army led by the Earl of Moray and Archibald Douglas at the Battle of Duppin Moor in Fife. He would be crowned King of the Scots at Scone in 1332. However he didn't have the backing of the whole of Scotland and, less than a year later, he fled south over the Border.

On hearing this Edward III tore up the "Treaty of Northampton" in which the right of Scotland to rule itself had been defined. Edward marched north to join forces with Balliol and proceeded to lay siege to Berwick with the inhabitants behind the town walls, bringing with him a number of siege engines to bring the town to its knees. Berwick held firm at first, despite Edward and Balliol's best attempts to make them surrender. Whilst the siege went on and the town held, a relief force of Scots managed to cross the River Tweed further west and move south-east to Tweedmouth, opposite Berwick on the south side of the Tweed and burn the town. This created a diversion and whilst it was in progress a force of about 200 managed to reinforce Berwick. The remainder of the Scottish force moved towards Bamburgh with the intention of laying waste to that area of north Northumberland.

Edward then made an agreement with the town that if 200 more Scots could breach his lines and reach Berwick by 20 July he would release all prisoners. Edward then positioned his army atop of Halidon Hill to the north-west of the town just off the road to Duns. By doing this Edward could survey the town and check in the direction he thought any attack by the Scots would come from. The army was arranged in three divisions with archers, Balliol commanding the left flank, Edward the centre, leaving the right flank to be commanded by Sir Edward Bohun.

The larger Scottish army reached the north side of Halidon Hill on the 19 July. The English army by this time had been encamped for a considerable time and suffered from both sickness and desertions, depleting the numbers.

The monument stone to the battle on the roadside on the road from Coldstream to Berwick.

The Scots were set up in three separate divisions and a separate force of 200 men, under the Earl of Ross, was left in reserve. It was the intention for this reserve force to move around the main battle and reach Berwick, to relieve the town. The Scots left flank was led by Archibald Douglas, the centre by Robert the Seward, and the right flank by the Earl of Moray. The Scottish grooms and some horses were positioned on Witches' Knowle a short distance away.

Prior to the Battle starting the Scottish champion, a giant of a man called Turnbull with an equally large black mastiff dog, stepped out from the Scottish ranks and challenged any man on the English side to man-to-man combat. An English knight called Robert Bahale accepted the challenge. The Scots expected Turnbull to win as Bahale was considerably smaller than Turnbull. The dog was the first to die, with Turnbull not long after with a short but fierce fight at the hands of Bahale's sword, the Scots losing their champion.

The Scots' first wave charged at the English, whose archers let loose a devastating volley of fire (a good archer of the time could accurately fire eight rounds a minute). Balliol's men despatched the few Scots to reach them, the archers taking a greater toll of the second and third waves of the Scots army. Ross, instead of circumnavigating the Battle, had to fight a rearguard action with his hand-picked men. The English knights mounted and chased the remnants of the Scottish army back to Duns.

The Battle didn't last very long and after it seventy Scottish lords, including Archibald Douglas lay dead, with them 7,000 men at arms. This was in contrast to the English army, which lost one knight and one man at arms in the battle. Edward Balliol was restored to the Scottish throne after the Battle, but was never accepted by the Scots.

This showed the way the English would fight over the next 100 years from Crecy to Agincourt, and the power of the English longbow.

Hell Beck (Gelt)
20 February 1570

The little River Gelt, said to have run red with the blood of the slain.

Fought upon either side of the little River Gelt, the Battle of Hell Beck is also known as the Battle of Gelt. The River Gelt and the battle site is not far from the Cumbrian town of Brampton.

The Battle itself was the final act in the "Rising of the Northern Earls" and the attempt by the Earls of Northumberland and Westmorland to place Mary, Queen of Scots on the throne of England and restore the Catholic faith in England. The failure to win the Battle led to the exile of Westmorland and the execution of Northumberland in York. It also effectively signed the death warrant for Mary, Queen of Scots.

The uprising started in 1569 when Charles Neville, Earl of Westmoreland and Thomas Percy, Earl of Northumberland rose up for the Old Religion and Mary, Queen of Scots who was being held by Queen Elizabeth I, a Protestant queen. Known often as "the Rising in the North" it was an ill-conceived and thought out campaign to overthrow the queen of England. The rebellion had the backing of Leonard Dacre of Cumberland, a noted Catholic sympathiser, who had 3000 men to call on.

Lord Scrope the warden of the English West March was worried that he would be invaded by Dacre's rebel force which was much greater than the garrison stationed at Carlisle Castle where Scrope had his command. Mary, Queen of Scots had been held at Carlisle and then moved for a time to Scrope's own castle of Bolton in Wensleydale. From there she was moved south to Sheffield Castle and then to Fotheringay for safety.

The rebel earls met and assembled their forces at Branspeth Castle near Durham; they marched on Durham and took the city, occupying the cathedral. They had then marched south as far as Bramham Moor in Yorkshire, with a force of some 4,000 men, proceeding then to the city of York. Fearing a larger army from the south the rebels retreated to Raby Castle and then to Barnard Castle, which they besieged. They laid siege to Barnard Castle, for eleven days before it surrendered under the command of Sir George Bowes. At this point they had a force of some 4,000 men and 600 horses, much smaller than the force of 7,000 that the Earl of Essex had gathered at York. The rebels then headed north, first to Auckland and then to Naworth Castle. There most disbanded after Dacre gave them a short period of shelter. After that the earls fled to Liddesdale in Scotland.

Yet Dacre was left with a problem when Queen Elizabeth found out about the double deal and his sheltering of the earls. Queen Elizabeth instructed Lord Hunsdon to meet the rebels and supress the rising, together with the old rogue Sir John Forster, who at the time of the Battle was nearly seventy years old. They rode forth from Newcastle to Hexham only thirty miles from Carlisle and Dacre's base at Naworth Castle.

The forces met in battle on the shores of the River Gelt. It was indeed a fierce and short battle with Dacre's force ultimately routed. It is said that the river ran red with the blood of the dead for several days after the Battle. Dacre himself fled to Scotland and then to Flanders, where he died in exile in 1575. Queen Elizabeth pardoned those borderers who fought with Dacre.

The Battle of Homildon Hill
14 September 1402

The Battlefield and Bendor stone with Homildon Hill behind.

The Battle of Otterburn remained in the mind of Henry Percy as a humiliating defeat by Douglas. As the political turmoil in England increased, the Scots took advantage of this in the best way they could, by raiding and reiving with Northumberland, taking the brunt of the action.

Henry IV had acquired the throne of England but by no means was he certain of the support from all his nobles; in fact plenty looked upon him as an imposter for murdering his cousin Richard II. His overtures to Robert II of Scotland for support fell on deaf ears, indeed it strengthened Robert's position to have an unsteady or weak king on the throne of England.

The Scots had also sided with the French who the English were at war with, it worried Henry that they may supply troops to Scotland. However it was a Scottish force under the Douglases led by Sir Archibald Douglas and backed by the Scottish government and supplemented with a few French troops that led a force into Northumberland in 1402. The force sacked most of Northumberland and reached as far as Newcastle, much as they had done in 1388, taking a considerable amount of plunder with them. The Scots then headed north towards the Border and home.

Percy, together with the Earl of March who like Percy had disagreements with Douglas, raised an army consisting of borderers and a considerable number of archers from Cheshire and Lancashire on behalf of the King. They then marched north to meet Douglas and intercept him on his way to Scotland. This time there would be no impetuosity from Percy, more of a calculated plan, using the traditional English fighting methods of the time.

The Scots, heavily weighed down with their booty, approached the Cheviots and within sight of the Border received intelligence that the English under Percy approached. So they pitched their camp on Homildon Hill just between the Cheviots and the River Till and the Millfield Plain. The English for their part approached the Scots army and positioned themselves on the opposite hill in full view, but out of range of anything the Scots could throw at them.

The English drew up their archers and let loose into the French ranks with volley upon volley falling without response. Indeed the French and Scots were unable to stop them, being totally unprotected on the slopes of the hill. The Scottish army was powerless, easy targets for the well trained English archers. The Scots took all they could take and charged the English lines. However, this exasperated the Scottish position as when they came onto the ground between the positions, the archers inflicted even more damage on the ranks of Scottish soldiers.

The Hotspur monument in Alnwick

This area of the battlefield around what is now known as the Bendor Stone is where much of the killing took place, with the Scottish casualties very heavy and the English exceptionally light. A number of the Scottish drowned in the Till trying to escape and a good many were captured, including Douglas himself.

The capture of the Scottish prisoners and the subsequent actions of Henry in seizing the prisoners for himself infuriated Percy. This soured the relationship between the two and the next year Percy joined Owain Glyndwr's rebellion, only to die in the Battle of Shrewsbury.

It can be said that this Battle was won purely by the English longbow, a forerunner to Agincourt some thirteen years later.

The Battle of Otterburn
5 August 1388

The field north of the village of Otterburn and beside the small copse where the Percy cross is standing, said to be the site of the battle.

When viewing the tranquil village of Otterburn today nestling in the beautiful Redesdale valley in western Northumberland, it is difficult to imagine the pitched battle that occurred here centuries ago, on the outskirts of the village we see today. This Battle is immortalised in not one but two ballads, the most notable being *Chevy Chase*.

The Battle of Otterburn was itself the culmination of one of the first large scale reiver raids chronicled. Set against a backdrop of war between the two nations for nearly a century, the battle was fought between two of the most prominent border families, one from each side of the Anglo-Scottish Border. On the English side The Percys, Earls of Northumberland. On the Scottish side the Douglases often known as the Black Douglases for their swarthy appearance and to distinguish them from the Red Douglases who resided further north, both families courageous and both very headstrong.

The Scots gathered a considerable force just south of Hawick in the Scottish borders. The raid was probably backed by the Scottish government of the time, no doubt in reprisal for the incursion into Scotland by Richard II in 1385. The main force split into two smaller forces, the larger contingent to proceed into Cumberland in the English West March and raid that area. The second, smaller contingent, was led by James the second Earl of Douglas, known by his supporters as the good Sir James, and to his enemies as the Black Douglas. This smaller force would head down the middle of Northumberland just inland so that they avoided the main strongholds of Bamburgh and Alnwick.

The English force at Alnwick was commanded by the Earl of Northumberland. His sons Sir Harry and Sir Ralph Percy commanded the force at Newcastle. Sir Harry (Henry) Percy, often known as Hotspur for his bold impetuosity, was immortalised in Shakespeare's *Henry III*. A further English force which would figure in this battle was mustered at Durham by Walter Skirlaw, the Bishop of Durham.

The Scots moved south through Northumberland, raiding and reiving until reaching the outskirts of Newcastle, having so far avoided a battle. The Scots appeared under the castle walls, and a challenge was issued by Douglas for a personal duel with Hotspur, a challenge that was accepted, the duel was then fought under the castle walls. During the fight Douglas captured Hotspur's pennon (standard). There followed some dialogue between the two protagonists, Douglas intimating a challenge to Hotspur to come and get his standard back at Douglas's castle in Scotland.

Douglas and his men then left Newcastle going west eventually hoping to join up with the larger force again. They headed up Redesdale past Elsdon and on to Otterburn, capturing Otterburn Tower on the way. The Scots camped for the night on the outskirts of Otterburn prior to heading back over the Cheviots to Scotland.

The Percys and Sir Matthew Redman gathered a force together to chase and overtake the retreating Douglas, yet the main force set off before the reinforcements under Walter Skirlaw could reach Percy at Newcastle. Percy's force made good time, for although he marched his men hard he arrived at Otterburn just before nightfall on 5 August. Most would have waited for daybreak and reinforcements, but true to his bold impetuosity Percy decided to attack, even with the encroaching darkness, despite the fact that the men were tired from the long march from Newcastle and the Bishop of Durham's reinforcements hadn't arrived. A tactical blunder and a surprising one, as most battles of that time were fought during daylight hours.

A Scottish sentry sounded the alarm in the camp just as most were partaking of supper. With the speed of Percy's advance Douglas did not have enough time to fully put on his battle armour. Percy drew up his force in battle order separated into two groups, the main group in front of the Scots camp and a second force under the control of Redman to the side of the Scots. Percy waited and watched while Redman attacked, making inroads into the Scottish flank.

Unknown to Percy, Douglas with the larger part of his force moved to the rear of the main section of Percy's force and attacked, surprising Percy's force. Thus at the onset of nightfall the Battle began with hand-to-hand combat. The English under Redman made significant headway in the early fray with Percy watching at a distance. That all changed with Douglas' flanking manoeuvre. In the late fourteenth century both areas spoke a common dialect and in a great many cases they would be unable to distinguish between friend and foe. This could have contributed to the heavy losses the English suffered, not helped also by tiredness and darkness.

In the heat of the Battle Douglas was mortally wounded and taken to under a bush or thicket with only his closest aides beside him including his two cousins, Sir John and Sir Walter Sinclair. Douglas made them promise that although he and they knew he was dying they would push on and keep it from the men. This they did, re-joining the battle shouting the cry "A Douglas, a Douglas!" as the rallying cry. This gave fresh impetus to the Scots and they pushed on until the fight had been won with both Sir Henry and Sir Ralph Percy captured along with 1,400 of their men. This brought to fruition the premonition that Douglas had had when he dreamed of a dead man winning the field.

The Percy Cross situated in a copse next to the Otterburn Battlefield.

The others fled the field and, on the road back to Newcastle, they met with the Bishop of Durham and his late reinforcements.

The Bishop, seeing the fleeing men and the affect it had on his own men, decided to withdraw when, if he had pressed home, the fight could have been won. The next day the Bishop would advance again and come to the same decision, not to engage the Scots rearguard. The Scots made their way over the Border with their prize. Both Sir Henry and Sir Ralph Percy were ransomed, with the English government paying part of the ransom.

Sir Henry Percy (Hotspur) would prove to be a thorn in the side of the Scots fourteen years later at the Battle of Homildon Hill near Berwick in 1402. He would die in the Battle of Shrewsbury in a rebellion against Henry IV the next year, 1403.

Douglas was taken home on a litter supported by his men and was buried at the small church within the grounds of Melrose Abbey.

Today the Percy Cross erected in 1777 stands in a small copse off the main road through Otterburn village. It's a stone cross replacing the original wooden one that stood on the same spot, overlooking the battlefield.

The Battle of Pinkie Cleugh
10 September 1547

The Roman Bridge at Inveresk, one of the few places to get heavy ordenance over the River Esk.

Henry VIII had started the War of the Rough Wooing in 1542, in order to marry his son Edward to the infant Mary, daughter of James V. When Henry died on 28 January 1547, the young Edward ascended to the throne of England as Edward VI. As Edward, at the time of his ascension, wasn't old enough to rule on his own, he needed a regent to rule for him. This position was filled by Edward Seymour, the maternal uncle of Edward, and Duke of Somerset. Somerset, under the title of Lord Protector, continued the Rough Wooing of Scotland for the marriage of Edward and Mary.

To this end Somerset invaded Scotland at the beginning of September 1547 with some 16,500 troops. These consisted of English border reivers, archers, billmen, German and Italian mercenaries together with cavalry. The army was led by Somerset himself, together with the Earl of Warwick and Lord Dacre of Gilsland, who probably commanded the reivers. The English sent a diversionary force west under the command of

Thomas Wharton, warden of the English Middle March, and the dissident Earl of Lennox. This diversionary force, of some 5,000 men, attacked and burned Annan in the Scottish West March.

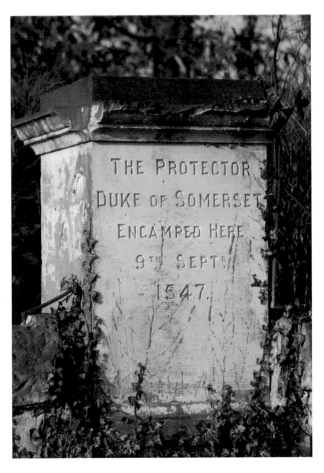

The stone monument to Somerset, however it has the wrong date. The army camped here on the 10th of September after the battle. The night before they camped a few miles away at Prestonpans.

The Scottish formed an army of some 20,000 men under the Earl of Arran, using Scottish reivers to harass the English army prior to the Battle. The Scottish army consisted of a large force of Highland pikemen under the command of the Earl of Angus. The Earl of Home commanded some 2,000 border cavalry. There were some English at that time who put the figure of the Scottish army at some 36,000 men.

Fa'side Castle near the point the English army occupied

The English had entered Scotland on the east coast and been shadowed all the way by a large fleet of some thirty English warships. They camped near Prestonpans on the night of 8 September. On the 9 of September, the thirty-fourth anniversary of Flodden, the first skirmishes of the Battle started. This was done by a chivalric challenge from the Earl of Home when, at the head of 1,500 light cavalry (all border prickers), he rode near the English camp and challenged them to equal combat. Lord Grey accepted this challenge reluctantly on behalf of Somerset and with 1,000 armoured men at arms and 500 more lightly armed lancers (probably English Reivers armed with the short lance). The English cavalry drove the Scottish cavalry back some three miles inland, which meant that when the main Battle started the Scots were missing a large proportion of their cavalry.

The English occupied the side of Falside Hill (now known as Fa'Side) where Fa'Side Castle now stands. The Scots occupied the slopes to the west bank of the Esk. On the morning of the Battle Somerset arranged his guns on the slopes of Inveresk, overlooking the Scottish position. The English then moved forward towards the village of Inveresk, only to find that the Scots had taken St Michaels Church. This meant they had abandoned a strong defensive position on the slopes on the Esk and became vulnerable to the English army. The Scots moved forward rapidly in shiltrons (bodies of tight troops in battle formation) to meet the advanced English cavalry. The Scots were successful against the cavalry in the battle formation as the compactness helped. Shiltrons were hard to break down and as a result the English cavalry suffered heavy losses.

However, the initial skirmishes with the cavalry meant that not only had the Scots lost the surprise element, but that they were now well within artillery range of both the English land guns and also those from the following ships. The artillery opened fire causing huge casualties in the Scottish ranks; some in the rear cut and ran. This should not have been a problem as they should still have had enough men and been defensively sound, with an earthen bank on their right flank and the Pinkie burn on their left. They had moved to within range of the English archers and arquebuses, which are small smoothbore firearms.

Having moved forward the Scots were now in full view of the English and in particular the naval gunners. Whilst the Scots had armaments, they had nowhere near the amount of the English nor could they reach the English ships. English artillery fired from all sides into the Scottish ranks with little or no reply. Under such heavy fire the Scottish could not remain where they were and tried to fall back out of the reach of the English artillery. This meant that the advanced part of the Scottish army doubled back through their own lines. This doubling back causing mayhem within the following Scottish ranks with men dropping their weapons whilst trying to flee from the onslaught of English guns. Ultimately this gave the English cavalry an opportunity to come back into the action and the retreat turned into a rout

Towards the end of the Battle the English set fire to Falside castle killing all that were left in the small garrison that had held out inside.

Some say the Scots were pursued all the way back to Edinburgh, quite some way from the battle site. Although the English won a crushing victory, they failed to get the prize they wanted: the marriage of Edward to Mary, with the Scots spiriting the infant to France, into the arms of the young Dauphin.

The Pinkie battle site as it stands today

The Raid of the Redeswire
7 July 1575

The Redeswire today looking north into Scotland

The last major battle of the time of the reivers between England and Scotland was in fact more of an affray than a pitched battle. However, where the reivers were involved it would be very hard to tell the difference. A day that started innocuously enough would end in a pitched battle between the English and the Scottish wardens and their respective followers. This incident happened on the English Scottish border at Carter Bar on the edge of the Cheviot Hills at the time in the Scottish Middle March.

Days of truce were held by the wardens at regular intervals on the borders, they were to sort out complaints from both sides with thieving, murders and other complaints all on the agenda. Some wardens on both sides got on well with each other and the business got sorted without major problems, other wardens didn't get on and in some cases hated each other. In these cases the truce

124

days often were postponed or cancelled due to either warden not being available.

On the day in question the Scottish contingent were led by Sir John Carmichael, deputy warden of the Scottish Middle March and, at the time, Keeper of Liddesdale. The English were led by Sir John Forster, warden of the English Middle March and a wily old fox. Forster had as his second in command Sir George Heron, the Keeper of Redesdale.

Large crowds gathered to follow each side and, as was also common on days of truce, stalls selling wares were set up near to the appointed place. With an amnesty being granted from sunrise on the day to sunrise on the next day, the atmosphere could be one of conviviality. However there could also be tension in the air as people on both sides would have an interest in the day's business, and old enemies could be watching on the other side.

The Redeswire stone, marking the battle site.

This time the proceeding started with the wardens hearing the complaints from both sides and passing judgement and sentence, where necessary. During the proceedings most things went well, until the case of Henry Robson of Tynedale was put before them, this case had been held over from the previous truce day, Robson being a noted reiver and freebooter. Forster had been requested to hand over Robson at the previous truce, and again was requested to produce Robson. Carmichael thought that Forster was stalling and double dealing, something Forster was noted for doing. Soon the insults began to flow from both sides and tempers flared.

As things deteriorated the Tyndale men started to release arrows into the Scottish ranks. Tables of the traders then began to be overturned and looted. With the Scottish contingent at first taking the worst of the battle and being pushed back down the hill. The men of Liddesdale then captured the English horses that were grazing nearby. As the Scots were pushed back down the hill they met with the Jedburgh men led by their Provost, who were arriving late for the proceedings. The cry went up from the Jedburgh men "a Jeddart, A Jeddart!" and they joined the fray, pushing the English back.

Both wardens tried to calm the fray, but to no avail. The followers would not be pacified and the fighting intensified.

After the Jedburgh men joined the fray the Scots regrouped to force the English back and pursued them back into England. In the fray Sir George Heron was killed and Sir John Forster captured along with other notable English officers. The English prisoners were taken to the Scottish Regent in Dalkeith, where after a few days they were released in accordance with the custom.

Sir John Carmichael at the request of the English parliament was sent to York, where he was questioned over his part in the affray. Sir John was cleared of any blame and freed with gifts from the English, in accordance with his rank.

The action is known as the "Raid of the Redeswire". However, it is neither a raid nor a battle, but it is remembered in Jedburgh and the borders.

The Battle of Solway Moss
24 November 1542

The River Esk at Longtown in Cumbria, the likely crossing point of the Scottish army in 1542

Henry VIII's protestations and arguments with the Catholic Church are well documented and in the early 1540s were in full flow. Henry invited his nephew James V of Scotland to join him against Catholicism. James for his part needed the church on his side as he had dealt with his nobles with a very heavy hand. James further infuriated Henry by refusing to meet him in York to talk about the situation.

Henry was furious at this rebuff by his nephew and sent an army north to invade Scotland. Laying waste to a considerable area of the Borders including burning the towns of Kelso and Roxburgh together with a number of the surrounding villages. This in turn enraged James who ordered Lord Maxwell, Warden of the Scottish West March, to raise an army with the intention of invading England.

The Scottish army of 20,000 men duly marched out of Edinburgh in November 1542 heading for the borders and ultimately to invade England from the west. James then split his army into two taking 10,000 men to Lochmaben, the other 10,000 under the control of James' favourite, Oliver Sinclair, headed directly for the Border and Longtown in Cumbria aiming to cross the River Esk at Solway Moss.

The English had advance warning of this and were prepared, albeit with a much smaller force, probably of around 3,000 men, consisting of mainly border horsemen with the short lance favoured in those parts, these were known as prickers, quick light cavalry. They were led by border wardens Sir Thomas Wharton and Sir William Musgrave, both experienced in border warfare and raiding, who moved towards the River Esk to meet the Scottish army.

The Scottish army unfortunately suffered from poor leadership and considerable infighting between the commanders. In that there was much resentment that the King had put Sinclair in charge. It wasn't a popular choice, making the army disorganised and uncoordinated. The King remained at Lochmaben throughout the Battle while the forward party crossed the Border, heading for the Esk. When the English force appeared before them it caused consternation and panic in the Scottish ranks, with the leaders unable to restore order.

The English hit hard and quick, making the most of the light cavalry. This scattered the Scottish ranks with the front turning and running into the rear. Whilst the Battle was quick and decisive the loss of life on both sides was very low for a battle at this time (low double figures on both sides) it is the number of prisoners taken by the English that is surprising, as many as 1,200. It is possible although undocumented that more Scots were drowned in the moss (a boggy waste to the north of the River Esk) itself while trying to flee the Battle.

The Battle had far-reaching consequences for the Scottish side, in that morale almost reached the same low depths as after the defeat at the battle of Flodden, some twenty-nine years earlier. After the defeat King James retreated back to Falkland Palace where he descended into the depths of depression and died two weeks later at the young age of thirty, leaving the infant Mary Stuart barely a week old. She would later become the ill-fated Mary, Queen of Scots.

Other Border Battles

Duns (1372)

Fought near the Berwickshire town of Duns, after which the Battle is named, this was indeed a victory for the local Scottish shepherds rather than an organised Scottish army. An English force led by Lord Henry Percy, Warden of the English East March crossed the Merse into Scotland on a raid. The force camped outside the town of Duns to await reinforcements from England overnight. The local shepherds, receiving information about the English encampment, gathered up the tools that they used to herd the sheep including rattles and skin drums. They made a noise with them as they encroached on the English encampment. The English, not knowing what the noise was, were scared and fled back over the Border, leaving their belongings in the camp.

Hadden Rig (24 August 1542)

This Battle was a precursor to the battle of Solway Moss later in November of the same year, but with the opposite results. Haddon Rig is situated three miles from the town of Kelso in Teviotdale. The 3,000-strong English army were led by Sir Robert Bowes, the 2,000 Scots by George Gordon 4th Earl of Huntley. The English incursion was the result of James V of Scotland refusing to meet Henry VIII at York, to discuss the marriage of his son Edward to James's daughter Mary. Little is known about how the Battle went, other than that it resulted in a resounding Scottish victory.

Melrose (25 July 1526)

This was an attempt by Sir Walter Scott of Buccleuch to secure the release of the young James V of Scotland from his regent Archibald Douglas, Earl of Angus. This was a bold attempt whilst the young king and his regent were travelling from

Jedburgh to Edinburgh. The Battle took place on the outskirts of Melrose, at a place called Skirmish Hill on the site of the Waverley Hotel. Against Scott stood the Kerrs of both Ferniehirst and Cessford and Robert Maxwell the 5th Lord Maxwell. Buccleuch charged with about 1,000 men mainly Scotts and Elliots, but the Kerrs held firm for the young king. During the Battle Andrew Kerr was killed by an Elliot who he was pursuing, when the Elliot turned and ran him through with his lance. This site is now marked by the Turn Again Stone.

Millerton Hill (1467)

The Battle site is situated off the B6355 road from Ayton to Chirnside. This Battle was a resounding victory for a Scottish army of 800 led by George Home of Wedderburn over the English army of 5,000 led by the Henry Percy, the 4th Earl of Northumberland.

Nisbet Moor (22 June 1402)

Scottish nobles led by Sir Patrick Hepburn of Hailes and Sir John Haliburton of Dirleton headed an incursion into England. They crossed the border into Cumbria with some 12,000 men, raiding and plundering the area around Carlisle. They then headed eastward into Northumberland and were heading back across onto Scottish soil in smaller groups. A band of the Scots army that had crossed met with an English force of some 200 men led by the exiled George de Dunbar the Earl of Dunbar and March. The result was a decisive victory for the smaller English force, the Scottish dead included Sir Patrick Hepburn. A larger Scottish force crossed the border later in 1402 and reached as far as the River Wear. They were ultimately defeated by Sir Henry Percy (Hotspur) at Homildon Hill.

Roxburgh, The Siege of (3 August 1460)

The English held Roxburgh, a royal castle. It was besieged by the nineteen-year-old King James II and a Scottish army. During the siege the King was visited by his Queen, Mary of Gueldress together with their infant son, soon to be James III. Whilst demonstrating the firing of one of the large cannon they had brought with them, the cannon blew up killing King James II. The Queen carried on the siege together with George, 4th Earl of Angus, the Castle surrendered soon after.

Sark (23 October 1448)

Also known as the Battle of the Lochmaben Stone, fought between the English, led by Henry Percy the future 3rd Earl of Northumberland and William Douglas, the 8th Earl of Douglas. Percy had taken some 6,000 men into Scotland, raiding in the borders. They made their army's overnight camp near to the town of Lochmaben, on a small plain near a tidal stretch of the little River Sark and the Kirtle Water. This position proved to be the English downfall, as when Douglas raised a border force of some 4,000 men assisted by Hugh Douglas, Earl of Ormond, to March against Percy. Although the English had the feared longbow, they were caught out by the rising tide and driven back by the Scottish spears.

Yeavering (22 July 1415)

A force of 4,000 Scots crossed into Northumberland while Henry V was occupied in France. They were met by a small English force of 400 consisting mainly of archers, led by Ralph Neville, 1st Earl of Westmorland. The Scots were well beaten, confirming, as did Agincourt in the same year, the power of the English longbow. There is a stone that marks the site of the battle.

Akeld Bastle
"The Little Fortlet"

Akeld Bastle is situated on a farm in the village of Akeld, just north of Wooler on the A697 in Northumberland. This two-storey fortified farmhouse from sixteenth century is in good condition. The stone steps at the end have been added at a later date (probably in the eighteeth-century rebuilding) to access the main doorway. The building was rebuilt and re-roofed in the eighteenth century, leaving only the ground floor as original. The ground floor has a vaulted ceiling in keeping with most bastle houses.

The house is first mentioned in 1522, when it was proposed by Lord Dacre to garrison ten men there. Surveyed by the border commissioners in 1541 it was described as a small fortlet or bastle without a barmkin, a fortified wall around the house. It is thought that the current wall that joins the house is of later construction. One of the striking things about this is its size; it is much larger than other bastle houses of the same time.

The house is no more than 500 metres away from the Bendor Stone, which marks out the site of the Battle of Homildon Hill in 1402. This was a crushing defeat for the Scots army.

Alnwick Castle
"The Windsor of the North"

Standing magnificently above the waters of the river Aln looking north towards Scotland is Alnwick Castle, often called "the Windsor of the North" painted by Canaletto, gardens designed by Capability Brown and home to the Dukes of Northumberland. It is indeed a magnificent sight, and these days a film star as well, with many credits to its name.

The Castle is not just a showpiece, although there is no doubt it's one of the finest in England. It has a rich and colourful past steeped in border and Anglo-Scottish history.

The first record of a castle at Alnwick was when it was besieged by an invading Scottish army led by Malcolm III (Canmore) and his son Edward in 1093. At that time the Castle and surrounding lands were held by the de Visci family, the area being controlled for the English King William Rufus (William II) by Robert de Mowbray, who was the incumbent of Bamburgh Castle a few miles north of Alnwick, on the coast. The Castle was besieged by Canmore after laying waste and besieging most of north Northumberland. At the time that area of the county would be as likely to be in either Scottish or English hands, as both laid claims to the lands in north Northumberland. Canmore had arrived at Alnwick on 13 November 1093, but before he and his army had time to settle into the siege they were attacked by Robert de Mowbray, Earl of Northumberland. The ensuing Battle led to the deaths of both Malcolm Canmore and his son Edward. They were later buried at Tynemouth Priory. A memorial stone marked the site of the Battle; this was replaced in 1774 by a stone cross, known locally as "Malcolm's Cross" it is situated in a small copse about a mile north of the Castle on the right-hand side of the old A1 Edinburgh road.

The Castle was captured in 1136 by King David I of Scotland. We must remember that at this point in time the Border as we know it didn't exist, so the taking of Alnwick was more of a land grab than an invasion. At the time of David's capture of the Castle it was in the hands of the de Vesci family. They still held the Castle when William the Lion of Scotland besieged it in 1172 and again in 1174 on two of his many raids into England to establish Northumberland as part of Scotland.

In 1212 the then custodian of Alnwick Eustace de Vesci was accused of conspiring with John Fitzwalter of Barnard Castle against King John of England. King John ordered the Castle to be destroyed, but for some reason that is not documented, his orders were not carried out.

The deVesci family died out in the late thirteenth century and the estates were passed to Anthony Bek, Bishop of Durham. The Percy or de Percy at the time purchased the Castle and its surrounding lands in 1309, thus starting a new chapter in the Castle's history. By this time the Border had been defined and Alnwick, together with the rest of Northumberland, was in England to stay. Within five years of Henry Percy acquiring Alnwick, Edward II had lost the Battle of Bannockburn to Robert the Bruce.

Malcolm's Cross, situated in a small copse on a hill north of the River Aln. To the memory of Macolm III "Canmore" who was killed at the Battle of Alnwick.

Henry Percy's original castle was a small stone affair of which I doubt that much, if any, remains. He began to build, expand and remodel his castle. His son Henry then continued the building to turn Alnwick into a major fortress in the north. Henry built the Abbotts Tower, Middle Gateway and the Constables Tower. The Percys acquired Warkworth in 1345 and for a time this became their preferred residence, one of the factors may have been that it was slightly further from the Border and therefore a bit safer, nevertheless Alnwick still remained prestigious. With this acquisition the Percys were becoming powerful in the North.

In 1403 after the first Earl of Northumberland, Henry Percy, had rebelled against Henry IV in the Battle of Shrewsbury and his famous son Harry Hotspur had been killed there, Henry besieged Alnwick. It only surrendered after a threat of using cannon to enter the Castle was made.

During the Wars of the Roses the Castle, like most in Northumberland, was held for the Lancastrian cause, surrendering in 1461 after the Battle of Towton. It then changed hands a number of times during the wars before finally surrendering to the Yorkist cause after the battles of Hedgeley Moor and Hexham in 1464.

In 1513 the English force under Surrey camped at Alnwick on their way to the Battle of Flodden field and a victory over the Scottish King James IV. For most of the sixteenth century Alnwick served as the administrative centre and base for the Warden of the English Middle March.

During the Rising of the Northern Earls in 1569, it was Thomas Percy the 6th Earl who rose up in support of Mary, Queen of Scots together with the Earl of Westmorland. A rebellion that was to end in failure and rout at Hell Beck in Westmorland. Thomas Percy, or Simple Tom as he was known, was captured after being on the run and executed in York in 1572. The Castle passed to his brother who became the 7th Earl and together with Sir John Forster held Alnwick for Queen Elizabeth.

Very little redevelopment happened to the Castle until the 4th Duke of Northumberland, Algernon Percy, rebuilt the Castle and employed Robert Adam to redesign large parts of it. It is due to the 4th Duke and Adam's work that it is the magnificent Castle we see today. Today the Castle is a major visitor attraction with its beautiful gardens. It is still a private residence for the current Duke of Northumberland and his family.

Ancroft Vicars Pele

The church of St Anne's is in the tiny Northumberland village of Ancroft just five miles south of the town of Berwick-upon-Tweed in what was the English East March. The church was built in the eleventh century, but it is unsure if it was before or after the Norman Conquest.

Built as one of four churches by the monks of Lindisfarne in their lands on the mainland, the others were at Lowick, Kyloe and Tweedmouth and sanctioned by Pope Eugenius III. On a clear day the island can be seen from the church tower.

The church when built had no tower. This was added in the fourteenth century when the priests needed protection from the increasing raids from over the Border. The tower built at the west end of the church contains the traditional arrow-slit windows common in a pele tower of this age where defence was a primary concern. This priest protection is in some ways unique as most were separate buildings, but like Edlingham Tower, the pele is built on to the church.

When the plague hit this area of Northumberland in 1667 Ancroft suffered at the same time, the dead from the plague were taken to a field and covered with broom and burnt, the field was and is still known as "Broomie Huts". The street where they lived, which would have been the main street at that time, was burnt as each family caught the plague and died. The field where the street was is just across the road from the church.

During the French Revolution at the end of the eighteenth century the church was connected with the estate of Haggerston Castle. Sir Carnaby Haggerston gave refuge to eight poor Clare sisters or nuns who fled the Revolution, they are buried within the churchyard and a gravestone erected in their honour.

For the first 450 years the priests were supplied by the Priory of Lindisfarne. Yet with the dissolution of the monasteries the supply of priests then fell to the Church of England and in particular to the Bishop of Durham until 1825, when the church passed into the Diocese of Newcastle.

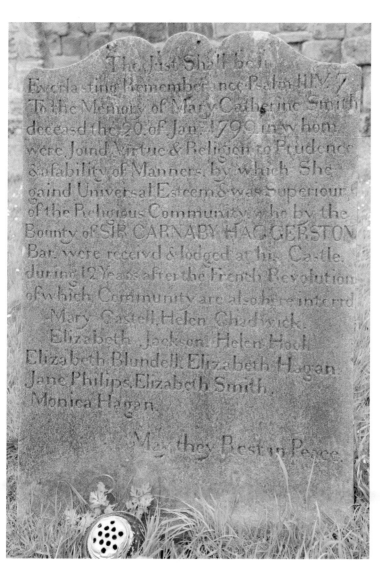

The Just Shall be in
Everlasting Remembrance Psalm III V 7
To the Memory of Mary Catherine Smith
deceasd the 20 of Jan 1799 in whom
were Joind Virtue & Religion to Prudence
& afability of Manners, by which She
gaind Universal Esteem & was Superiour
of the Religious Community who by the
Bounty of SIR CARNABY HAGGERSTON
Bar. were receivd & lodged at his Castle
during 12 Years after the French Revolution
of which Community are also here interrd
Mary Castell, Helen Chadwick,
Elizabeth Jackson Helen Hook
Elizabeth Blundell Elizabeth Hagan
Jane Philips Elizabeth Smith,
Monica Hagan.

May they Rest in Peace

The gravestone to the French nuns.

Aydon Castle
"A Converted Manor"

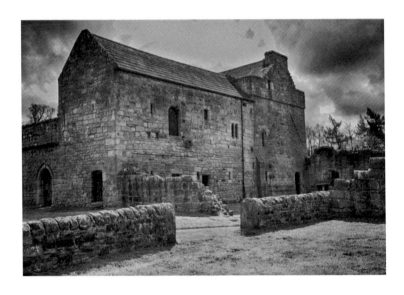

This was built as a manor house in the late thirteenth century by Robert de Raymes (buried at Bolam Church) a wealthy Ipswich merchant. Robert purchased the land from another Suffolk merchant Hugh de Gosbeck, who had inherited the land through his wife. The land and some of the surrounding area amounted to half the barony of Bolam, the other half being sold through inheritance many years previously.

Robert was indeed rich and served as a knight in the borders, fighting in Scotland for Edward I then fighting and being captured at Bannockburn in 1314, his ransom set at 500 marks equating to £333. He fought again in Scotland and later served as one of two members of Parliament for the county of Northumberland.

As a manor the house had a great hall, this was fortified with an outer wall by Robert and then he was given a licence to crenellate by Edward I in 1305. This would be for both practical reasons, against attack, and as a status symbol to show off his considerable wealth and standing. Robert married well to Maud Wortley, connected to the Heron family of Ford Castle, to become one of the Northumberland gentry.

The ascension to the Scottish throne in 1306 of Robert the Bruce and the death of Edward I a year later put the borders into fresh turmoil. With the Scots raiding Northumberland with increased frequency and in 1311 and 1312 the area around Aydon was laid waste. Aydon was not spared by the forces of Robert the Bruce. In 1315 after Bannockburn the Castle fell again to Bruce when Hugh de Gales meekly surrendered to the Scots whilst looking after the Castle for Robert de Raymes in his absence.

The main hall of Aydon Castle

Aydon continued to suffer like most of Northumberland during the next two centuries with border raids becoming more frequent. The Castle passed firstly to Robert's son, also called Robert and then to his grandsons. The youngest, Nicholas was imprisoned for some years for his part in the murder of John Coupland, a government official who was widely despised. Nicholas came into possession of Aydon in 1376. Nicolas was well connected to Henry Percy the first Earl of Northumberland and would have known the young Hotspur. Nicolas died in 1394, none the worse for his adventures and still in possession of the Castle.

Whilst in 1415 the Castle was reported as still in good order, by 1450 it had been reported that it was in a ruinous state. This was in part due to the fall in the fortunes of the de Raymes family as they appeared to lose their wealth in the early part of the fiftteenth century. Aydon was still occupied throughout this time until the sixteenth century when the 8th Robert de Raymes handed the Castle to Sir Richard Carnaby in exchange for other lands. Sir Richard gave the Castle to his brother Cuthbert. Cuthbert made substantial changes to the Castle, including a kitchen and latrine block in 1540.

By 1612 the Castle had been let to tenants, one Lionel Winshoppe. Ralph Carnaby supported Charles I during the Civil War and due to this was penalised heavily after the war, causing the castle to be sold again. Eventually the Castle was acquired by the Blackett family who held it until recently. Today, the castle is cared for by English Heritage.

Bamburgh Castle
"Castle of Kings"

Bamburgh is probably one of the most photographed castles in the British Isles and it's not difficult to see why. Built from Red Sandstone and perched high on its grey basalt outcrop it appears like a sentry on duty. Bamburgh Castle stands majestically looking out on the North Sea, guarding its charges in the beautiful village of Bamburgh below. It is almost the perfect setting for a Castle, the high position giving it a magnificent defensive view over the surrounding countryside and any approaching army.

The earliest fortification here is first recorded in 547 and then became the original home of the kings of Northumbria from the seventh century. A small wooden fort stood on the same ground, protected by, according to Bede, nothing but a hedge. The present Castle's construction was begun in the eleventh century for Robert de Mowbray under the careful eye of Master Elias. Elias had studied under Master James of St George who built the castles in Wales for Edward I. In this light it is no wonder that Bamburgh became the magnificent castle we see now – it was not, however, without its ups and downs.

After Robert's wife surrendered the Castle to Henry II in order to stop the King gouging out Robert's eyes, Henry then had the wonderful keep built that housed the great hall of the Castle and expanded it to cover some five acres. The Castle then became a stronghold for the English during the Border wars between England and Scotland.

During the Wars of the Roses Bamburgh, along with Alnwick and Dunstanburgh, held firm for the Lancastrian cause. The Castle stood firm until 1464 when it was besieged for nine months by Richard Neville, the Earl of Warwick. At the end of the siege, canons were used to break down the walls of the Castle, thus becoming the first castle in the UK to have its walls broken and defeated by artillery.

Bamburgh sadly lay in ruins after this defeat until Queen Elizabeth I gave the Castle to Sir John Forster and his family who were wardens of the English Middle March. It remained in the Forster family for twelve generations until Sir William Forster died in 1700 and was declared bankrupt, posthumously. His estates, including Bamburgh, were sold to Lord Crewe, the Bishop of Durham, who was married to Sir William's sister Dorothy, which settled the debts.

The Castle was still in poor condition but successive owners continued to improve and repair the structure. Finally at the end of the ninteeth century the Castle was bought by the armaments industrialist Lord Armstrong. The Armstrong family still own Bamburgh to this day.

The grounds of the Castle have been examined many times by archaeologists, most notably in the 1960s. During this period Dr Brian Hope-Taylor unearthed what has become known as the Bamburgh Sword. This sword is dated from the Anglo-Saxon period where an older fortification stood on this site. Some think that the sword may have even belonged to King Oswald of Northumbria.

The sword disappeared for many years finally being found by a student in a suitcase in the garage of Brian Hope-Taylor's house, after his death in 2005. The sword has thankfully been returned to the Castle, where it is on display.

Barmoor Castle
"The Rest before Flodden"

The land to the west of Lowick and what was once the village of Barmoor were granted to Robert de Muschampe by Henry I as part of the barony of Wooler. Robert built a tower or pele here, this in turn helped the village grow from the tower out. The de Muschampe family had followed William the Conqueror here after 1066 and settled in the lands of north Northumberland near Wooler.

Stephen de Muschampe granted some of the lands from his estate at Barmoor to the monks of Lindisfarne in exchange for burial rights within the Priory in 1221, this would appear to ensure the burial rights for future de Muschampes as well as himself.

In 1291 Edward I visited Barmoor, probably on his way to Norham to listen to the Great Cause for the Scottish throne. It is not recorded how long Edward stayed at Barmoor on his way north, or indeed if he stopped again on the return south.

In 1319 the Muschampe family again played host to royalty when Edward II visited Barmoor on his way north to relieve Berwick, which had been taken by Robert the Bruce and was being held by the Scots.

Licence to crenellate was granted to Thomas de Muschampe on 17 May 1341 by Edward III at Westminster. This added battlements, arrow-slit windows and gun-loops to the existing structure to fortify it against Scottish raids.

Henry V gathered his wardens of the Marches and an army of 100,000 at Barmoor in 1417 to march against the Scots. They had crossed the Tweed heading south into Northumberland. On hearing of Henry's army the Scots dispersed without entering into a battle.

On 8 September 1513, the night before the battle, Thomas Howard, Earl of Surrey camped here with his army en route to Flodden and the defeat of James IV and the Scottish army. A year later it was reported that the Castle could hold thirty knights, yet by 1548 they could only muster seven able men and the Castle had fallen into decay. A report on the state of the Castle produced in 1550 described it as very "cast down". George Muschampe did do repairs to the property in 1584 to try and repair some of the damage. It must have suffered during reiving times and repeated raids from over the Border.

The Civil War found the Muschampes on the side of King Charles I. This left the estate somewhat impoverished, as there was retribution by Parliament against those who supported the King. On 23 February 1649 Lady Muschampe declares administration in favour of her husband's creditors after his death. Two years later the Castle passed to the Carr family of Etal. Some more restoration work was done at this time up until the 1680s.

The Castle passed through various hands until it came into those of Francis 'Frank' Sitwell in 1791. He employed noted Edinburgh architect John Paterson to modernise and restructure it into a Gothic-style town house. Starting the work in 1801, later improvements were done in 1892 by Brigadier-General W. H. Sitwell.

Today the Castle is a centrepiece for a holiday park.

Berwick Castle
"The Forgotten One"

The water tower of Berwick castle standing alongside the River Tweed.

Standing on the north bank of the River Tweed are the remains of Berwick Castle, a sad demise to a once great and important border fortress. With walls up to fifty feet high and twelve feet thick it was an impressive sight. Not much remains of the castle where Edward I declared for John Baliol as the Scottish King in 1292. The west curtain wall, constable's tower and the breakneck stairs are all that exist today, these parts date from the thirteenth century.

King David I of Scotland first built a castle in Berwick on the steep slopes of the Tweed to watch his southern border. Through the years it had a chequered history passing from English hands to Scottish hands and back, and with the Castle the whole town often changed hands. It has to be said that not all were bloody battles and sieges. In 1199 Richard I, the Lionheart, sold the Castle to the Scottish in order to pay for the Third Crusade.

Edward I sacked the town on Good Friday 1296 when the Castle commanded by Sir William Douglas, its commander, refused to surrender. Edward's men put some 7,500 souls to the sword taking two days to complete the task and sparing no one, men, women or children in an act of barbarity that stands out even in those times of brutality. After the massacre Edward had the Castle and town defences rebuilt and strengthened.

The Castle became English for the last time in 1482 during the Wars of the Roses when Richard, Duke of Gloucester captured it from Patrick Hepburn, Lord Hailes. The Castle and town having changed hands no less than thirteen times between 1296 and 1482.

During the fifteenth and sixteenth centuries Berwick Castle was the administrative centre and base of the Warden of the English East March. Sir Robert Carey grew up here when his father Lord Hunsdon was the warden; he himself was the warden when in September 1596 he hanged the noted Reiver Geordie Bourne.

The building of the new ramparts during the reign of Elizabeth I made the Castle outdated and, while it was used for the remainder of her reign for administrative purposes, some of the Castle and its stone were used for the new walls. The Castle fell into ruin after the Union of the Crowns in 1603. The final demise came with the arrival of the railway and the building of the Royal Border Bridge in 1847-1850, when stone from the Castle was used to build the station. The station stands where the magnificent great hall stood and Edward I presided over the future kings of Scotland.

The remains and the ramparts are cared for today by English Heritage.

Berwick's Elizabethan Walls

Holding a strategic place on the Border and indeed the only port on either side of the border marches, Berwick was prized by both Scotland and England. Indeed Tudor thinking in England held it as strategically important as Calais, an importance that escalated when they finally lost Calais in 1558 after a siege.

As the sixteenth century rolled on the castle in Berwick waned it still held the seat for the Warden of the East March but its strength was not what it had been in earlier centuries. Thinking turned towards how Berwick and indeed that area of England's northern border could be protected and strengthened, a seaborne attack was always in the back of the mind of Elizabethan thinking.

Plans had been drawn up for stronger defences in the early 1550s but this escalated when Queen Mary married Philip of Spain. Spain at that time was at war with France, a not uncommon state for England to be in. France on the other hand was both an old ally and old enemy of England. This presented a problem in that an invasion could be mounted on Berwick.

The fall of Calais in January 1558 hastened the advancement in the defences at Berwick, earlier modifications to defences built by Edward I proving manifestly unsuitable. The new defences were to be of an Italian style; Queen Elizabeth, who was noted for being tight fisted with the royal coffers was persuaded that this was in England's best interests and sanctioned the building of the walls. The plan was commissioned from the Italian designer Portarini, with Sir Richard Lee as surveyor in charge of construction. The walls cost £128,648 an astronomical cost in the middle of the sixteenth century which must have choked the royal purse. But certainly cheaper than another scheme put forward, which was to build a Hadrian-like structure the length of the Border.

Even today the walls are a masterpiece of engineering. With the threat of armaments in the forefront, the thinking behind the walls' construction so that they would resist serious cannon fire, with the earthen filled walls reaching thirty feet in thickness in some places. Added to the thickness there are five landward-facing bastions, pointed and joined by a curtain wall. With cannon placed either side it would have been difficult for any infantry to get close to scaling the walls without being strafed by shot. Outside the walls and bastions are large water-filled ditches, the water is no longer visible.

These walls when completed in 1570 made Berwick almost impregnable and are some of the best preserved town defences anywhere in the British Isles. Whilst they are known as the Elizabethan walls or ramparts they were however started or commissioned by Queen Mary before her death in November 1558.

Today the walls are in the care of English Heritage and can be walked at any time of year.

Bewcastle Castle

Bewcastle Castle stands on a mound at the north end of the farming community of Bewcastle in Cumbria, just inside the English borders looking out over the Bewcastle waste, it was a garrison fortress at the time of the reivers. Now no more than a shell of what was, a stronghold in the borders against the raiding parties.

The original castle was started in the eleventh century and built where a Roman fort once stood, in all probability using some of the remains of the old Roman fortifications. It would more than likely have been constructed substantially of timber in a motte and bailey type of layout.

The present stone castle was built around 1340 to 1360. This Castle was given to John de Strivelyn, a general to Edward III. Later the Castle passed into the Middleton family, under whose ownership it fell into disrepair. In the fourteenth century Edward IV gave the Castle to his brother the Duke of Gloucester, Later Richard III; around 1478 he then substantially repaired it.

It was further strengthened in the fifteenth and sixteenth centuries whilst garrisoned against the reivers. During the late sixteenth and early seventeenth centuries it was held by the

Musgrave family, who were constables of the Castle. By the middle of the sixteenth century it had again fallen into disrepair and was in a ruinous state, to be garrisoned for the last time in 1639.

Black Middens Bastle
"Fortified Farmhouse"

Bastle houses are found along the English border with Scotland. Named after the French prison, the Bastille, they are fortified farmhouses of the fifteenth and sixteenth century. They were owned and protected by the powerful farming reiver families and their more important livestock, when raids from over the Border happened. The family would reside in the upstairs with the cattle being housed, when a raid was on, in the downstairs.

Black Middens Bastle is situated in the Tyne Valley, surrounded by the beautiful Northumberland countryside and in the peace and tranquillity of today it gives no hint of its turbulent past. A traditional bastle house, it has outer stairs to the living quarters and small windows for a defensive strategy.

The two lower door entrances on Black Middens are later eighteenth-century additions to the original structure. The stairs are also a later addition as during reiving times the entrance would be through wooden steps that would have been removed indoors during a raid.

There are the remnants of two bastle houses on this site and the ruins of a newer farmhouse, although all three are now deserted. They are in the care of English Heritage.

Brough Castle
"Clifford's Retreat"

Perched on a hillock just outside of the village of Brough in what was Cumberland and next to what is the A66 trans-Pennine road is Brough Castle. Like Brougham a few miles north-west on the A66, it was owned by the same two families, the de Vieuxponts and the Cliffords.

The oldest part of this Castle was actually built by William Rufus, son of William the Conqueror in around 1100, these are the north and south curtain walls nearest the keep. He built the original castle when he annexed what is now Cumbria from Scottish rule. The initial structure was the keep with a wooden palisade. The keep at that time had a masonry base and a main tower structure of wood. The ground the Castle covers is thought to be much the same as the ruins in which the later structure, seen today, stands.

The annexation of the lands didn't go down well with successive Scottish kings. They made repeated attempts to reclaim the land, putting Brough in the firing line of various raids and skirmishes. William the Lion of Scotland led raids into Cumberland in both 1173 and 1174. He blockaded Carlisle and laid waste to Brough. Chroniclers tell of Brough being defended by six knights complete with their retinues. Which probably doesn't sound much but the retinue of a knight would be a considerable number of men at this time. The attackers set fire to the keep, which was largely wooden, in order to get the knights to surrender. One of the knights held out for a considerable length of time at some cost to the invading Scottish force.

The keep at Brough Castle

The stone base that the old wooden keep had been built on provided an ideal base for a new keep made of stone, in all probability the one we see today. In 1203 King John gave the Barony of Brough and Appleby to Robert de Vieuxpont (Vipont), who at that time had built Brougham Castle. The Castle for the next few years fell into decay, but was restored prior to 1268 when Robert Clifford acquired it. He would have entertained Edward I when he stayed at both Brough and Brougham on his way north to Scotland, in 1300.

Brough was in a disputed area between England and Scotland and ruled by both at different times, until the Border was finally defined in the Treaty of York in 1237, bringing it under English rule. The town was raided again by the Scots after Bannockburn in 1314, laying waste to the town, but they left the Castle undamaged. They raided the town and Castle again in 1319 yet this time the Castle stood firm, having at this time a larger garrison of some fifteen men at arms as well as both heavy and light cavalry.

During the Great Scottish Raid of 1388 led by Sir James Douglas and culminating in the Battle of Otterburn, Brough and the neighbouring castle at Appleby were sacked as the Scottish army returned to Scotland. Around this time Sir Roger Clifford made substantial changes to the inside of the Castle, building the hall on the first floor between Clifford's tower and the gatehouse. It would have appeared to be a family favourite as they frequently stayed here on their visits to the area.

During the Wars of the Roses the area of Westmorland was unaffected, but Thomas Clifford fought for Henry VI, falling at the Battle of St Albans in 1455. The Cliffords re-established their residence at Brough around 1485 after the war had ended. In 1521 Sir Henry Clifford held his Christmas celebrations at Brough, where unfortunately a fire broke out during the celebrations destroying all the woodwork and decoration throughout the castle. It was then abandoned as a residence until Lady Anne Clifford inherited the Castle in around 1643.

Although the wooden artefacts and decorations were destroyed by the fire the stonework and masonry appears to have been structurally sound, so Lady Anne set about rebuilding and decorating the Castle. This she did, after the Civil War had ended, starting the rebuild around 1659. Some of the restoration she documented in her diary:

1660: "This castle and the Roman Tower in it was so well repaired by me at my exceeding great cost and charge".

1662: "This summer did I cause to be built a kitchen, bake house and brew house and a stable in the court of my castle at Brough".

An entry recorded in 1666 reports of a fire in the Round Tower being a setback to the restoration. After her death in 1676, the new owners were not so enthusiastic about Brough and it fell into neglect. It was in a decaying state by 1695 when the keep was reported to be gutted. A large part of the round tower was removed in 1763. Today, it is a shell of what it would have been in its heyday. The Castle is in the care of English Heritage.

Brougham Castle

Beautifully situated just above the River Eamont in Cumbria, the ruins of Brougham Castle stand proudly where they once defended the English border and entertained kings. Dating from the early part of the thirteenth century before the major hostilities between England and Scotland. The castle was built by one of King John's most trusted advisors, Robert de Vieuxpont. The land was given to him in order that he defend King John's kingdom from its enemies in the north.

In all likelihood the first castle here would have had a stone keep, which is still in evidence today, with an outer timber palisade. The timber would be replaced in later years by stone walls which were more substantial. In 1268 the Castle passed into the Clifford family by way of marriage of one of the de Vieuxpont girls to Robert Clifford. The rise of the Castle came a few years later in 1296 with the Scottish wars of independence, when Robert Clifford was Warden of the West March for King Edward I. Indeed, Edward I stayed at Brougham Castle in 1300 on his way to the siege of Caerlaverlock Castle. The outer walls and bailey were strengthened at this time. Brougham was the Cliffords' main residence, even though they held other castles such as Skipton and Brough.

Little is known about the next eighty years until the 5th Lord Brougham made changes, including a number of new buildings, along the south wall. In 1388 around the time of the Battle of Otterburn the Castle was sacked and taken by the Scottish.

The keep at Brougham Castle

The Castle assumed importance once again when the Cliffords sided with the Lancastrian cause during the War of the Roses against the Yorkist Nevilles. John Clifford was killed fighting for Henry VI in 1461, after this the King gave the Castle to the Nevilles, who were the earls of Westmoreland. Brougham was later back in Clifford hands when Henry Clifford, John's son, was granted Brougham and the rest of his family's lands from Henry VII. This started one of the most prosperous periods for Brougham and the Clifford family. The Tudor court was good in the early years but, by later times when George Clifford, the 3rd Earl of Cumberland found himself more and more in the south at the court of Queen Elizabeth I (in his role as queen's champion), the Castle unfortunately went into a period of decline and neglect until the death of George in 1605.

George's widow, Margaret, revived the Castle's fortunes so much that King James I stayed here and was lavishly entertained in 1617. Unfortunately Margaret didn't live to see the royal visit as she died in 1616.

During the Civil War the Castle operated as a royal garrison. At the end of the war, George's daughter, Lady Anne Clifford, restored the Castle and laid out a substantial garden. After Lady Anne's death in 1676 the Castle was maintained for a while, but then fell into disrepair. The 6th Earl of Thanet disposed of large parts of the fixtures and fittings of the Castle, preferring to live at Appleby Castle. Sadly for such a majestic castle in a beautiful setting, Brougham fell into ruins with no roof and crumbling walls. In 1928 the Castle was handed over to the Ministry of Works.

Today Brougham is in the guardianship of English Heritage.

Carlisle Castle
"Buccleuch Dares, Kinmont Wins"

The largest castle in the western marches, Stanwix castle in Carlisle is a magnificent fortress even today and has served, in various capacities, for nearly 900 years. The Castle was built by William Rufus, the son of William the Conqueror, on the site of the old Roman fort of Stanwix on the northern side of Carlisle with a south-facing gateway. In all probability the structure would have been constructed largely of wood with an outer wooden palisade, it was situated near a ford on the River Eden.

Rufus built the castle after retaking the town and driving Malcolm III (Canmore) out of Cumberland and re-establishing English rule over the county. He realised the importance, in military terms, of a castle and a garrison here on the north-western border with Scotland. The problem with the wooden castles and palisades is the use of fire against them. So later, in the reign of Henry I, the wooden structure was replaced by a stone castle with an inner and outer bailey. We know that the keep of the current Castle dates, at its oldest, from the late twelfth century. The keep was completed in stone by David I as the Castle was by then back in Scottish hands where it stayed until

1157 when David I died in it. Henry II reclaimed both the Castle and the rest of Cumberland, so that it came back under English control. One of the main reasons for the Scottish being able to take the Castle and indeed most of Cumberland is that during King Stephen's reign his battle with Empress Maud consumed his time and focus, thus leaving the Scots and indeed the north in general to its own devices.

During the reign of Henry III in 1237 the Treaty of York established the Border and finally brought Carlisle permanently into England. It didn't stop the Scots from trying to recapture it.

Edward I strengthened the Castle and used it on a number of occasions in his attempt to subdue Scotland. He actually held parliament within the Castle in 1306-7 just before his death at Burgh on Sands. Unlike his father Edward II was not a great soldier and lost the Battle of Bannockburn to Robert the Bruce in June, 1314. The following year Bruce laid siege to Carlisle Castle, throwing all he had at the siege, yet he couldn't break the Castle defences and it stood firm. The Scots left after eleven days after laying waste to some crops and driving off the cattle round the Castle.

The Castle's defender at the time was Sir Andrew de Harcla. He was rewarded handsomely for the defence by Edward II, yet the next year he was accused of treason and executed as a traitor with his parts being displayed at London Bridge, Newcastle, Shrewsbury, York and Carlisle.

The Castle was then neglected for some considerable time; however, in 1538 Henry VIII made significant alterations. These were in response to the growing diplomatic crisis abroad and his war with France and indeed to problems at home after "the Pilgrimage of Grace" in 1536. Strengthening was needed to keep good order in the north. Four years later he added the half-moon gun batter at the base of the Captain's Tower where it forms the entrance to the inner bailey.

Under Elizabeth's reign and after her capture in 1568 Mary, Queen of Scots was first held in Carlisle Castle. Arriving at the Castle on 18 May 1568 and leaving two months later on 13 July, she was held in the Warden's Tower and frequently walked along what is known as Lady's Walk situated just in front of the south curtain wall.

The Castle was thought of as a major fortress during the Elizabethan period and came under the control of Thomas Lord Scrope, yet in 1596 it was the setting for one of the most daring raids and escapes in the reivers period. William Armstrong of Kinmont was imprisoned in the Castle walls. Until, this is, 13 April 1596 when a party of Scottish reivers led by "the Bold Buccleuch" entered the Castle by a postern gate and freed Kinmont from his cell. They probably had a good deal of inside information about the Castle and the escape led to some red faces within the Castle hierarchy and a diplomatic row between England and Scotland.

The Half Moon gallery built during the reign of Henry VIII.

With the Union of the Crowns in 1603, the ascension to the throne of James VI of Scotland to become James I of a United Kingdom opened up a new chapter for the Castle. James's reign was relatively peaceful except for the rounding up of noted reivers and freebooters in its first few years while he effectively cleansed the borders.

It was during the reign of his son and successor Charles I where the problems for Carlisle rose again. Charles effectively alienated the Scottish, religiously, and with the rising in Ulster the need to strengthen Carlisle Castle was apparent. The Castle had new gun batteries built in the south-west and north-west portions of the outer bailey, seeing to it that Carlisle would once again become a major garrison for the crown during the Civil War that followed. In October 1644 an army of Scots surrounded the Castle and dug in for a long siege. The King's garrison was however in good heart and were equally prepared to sit it out. The siege lasted eight months, only to end it when the King's cause was lost. The Cavaliers marched out of the broken town and Castle on 28 June 1645.

Carlisle Castle became a royal fortress again in 1660 with the ascension of Charles II to the thrones of both England and The Protestant Charles was followed on the throne by his Catholic brother James II, who was uncompromising in his religious views and, in a throwback to the constant changing of Tudor times, religion was at the forefront. James II however fled the country in November 1688 not long after the birth of his son, also called James, who would become known as "the Old Pretender". He was replaced on the throne by the Protestant William III and Mary.

During the rebellion of the Old Pretender in 1715, Carlisle remained untouched with the cause missing Carlisle on their way south. It wasn't the same in the 45 rebellion under Bonnie Prince Charlie. Previous Scots armies had favoured the east-coast route, but there was a strong and well garrisoned fortification at Berwick, Carlisle on the other hand was only lightly garrisoned and Bonnie Prince made it a prime target to capture Carlisle and its castle. This they did with ease as the Hanoverian army under Marshall Wade was garrisoned at Newcastle upon Tyne and didn't have time to march west to strengthen Carlisle. Charles didn't reside in Carlisle long, leaving the next day to march south until he reached just north of Derby. The King's son, the Duke of Cumberland, often known as "Butcher Cumberland", lost no time moving north and pushing the retreating Scots army. When he reached Carlisle the Castle had only a small garrison and, after bombardment followed by a short siege, they surrendered. The Castle was then used as a prison, some of the garrison were hung and some banished overseas.

The Castle then became almost a permanent garrison, with rioting later in the century and again in 1828. Over the next two centuries barracks were added inside the outer bailey. This culminated in the formation of the Border Regiment in 1881, they would have their headquarters in the Castle. In 1959 the Regiment left for the last time and the Castle wasn't used as a barracks again.

Today Carlisle Castle is administered and looked after by English Heritage. There is also a wonderful underpass from the Castle to the Tullie House Museum and the underpass is decorated with the engraved family names of the border reivers.

Chillingham Castle

Nestled against a backdrop of the Cheviot Hills, Chillingham is in a beautiful setting, known today for its white cattle and as one of the most haunted castles in the UK. The Castle is in a strategic position in relation to the English-Scottish border, lying only a few miles north of Chillingham in the Cheviots.

Originally the site the Castle was designated for a monastery, as there were two castles nearby at Wooler. However this changed when the Grey family took over the estate in 1246, who fortified the site against the Scots. In 1247 royal permission was granted to crenellate and enclose the park to make it a hunting park, this included fencing in the white cattle that survive wild in the park to this day. The herd is about 100 strong and cannot be driven or herded, they are truly wild. No record exists to say if, during the reiving times of Elizabeth, any of the cattle had been taken, even though the Castle would have been attacked on numerous occasions.

King Edward I stayed at the Castle in 1298 on his way north to Scotland to do battle with William Wallace. In 1344 King

Edward III granted the licence to crenellate the manor house which made it into a full castle, to protect England's northern border.

The Chillingham wild white cattle.

During the Elizabethan period Chillingham was designated to be mustered with the Middle March; however Lord Hunsdon preferred it to be mustered with the East March when he was in charge of the East March from Berwick. In 1513 when James IV marched south to invade England and his fate at Flodden Field, Chillingham was one of the castles taken by the Scots. It is not understood whether it was stormed or besieged, either way it could not have held out for long against a large Scottish army. The Scots then set about dismantling the Castle, a task they probably didn't finish as it was handed back to the Grey family after the battle.

By the Union of the Crowns at the start of the seventeenth century the Castle, or at least the fortifications, weren't required, so the noted designer Inigo Jones was hired to modernise the Castle back to a manor house. In 1617 James I and VI stayed in the Castle on one of his many journeys between Edinburgh and London. Around this time the moat was filled in and there were residential areas built around the old battlements.

During World War II the Castle was used as a barracks for troops, some of the timber lining the walls was stripped and used to keep the troops warm during the cold north-east winters. This led to the Castle falling into a state of disrepair. This was the state of the Castle until 1982, when Sir Humphrey Wakefield the 2nd Baronet acquired the Castle, through his wife Catherine, who is descended from the original owners, the Grey family. Together they set about restoring the Castle and its Italian garden to its present glory.

Today the Castle is a tourist attraction and large sections are open to the public, approved for weddings and other functions. The cattle are still to be seen, however they are run separately by the Chillingham Cattle trust.

Corbridge Vicars Pele

Not all of the church pele towers were constructed as part of the church. Some, like the one at Corbridge, were separate and in the grounds of the churchyard. Built in 1319, it is one of the earliest Pele towers and probably one of the oldest still standing. First recorded in papers as a fortification against Scottish raids in 1415 in a list of fortifications drawn up for Henry V, the tower stands in the grounds of St Andrews Church in the centre of Corbridge village.

Constructed of sandstone measuring twenty-seven feet by twenty-one and thirty feet in height, the stone most likely came from the Roman remains at Corstopitium local to Corbridge. The tower covers three floors with bartizans in each corner and was refuge for the priest and villagers during the reiving times. The roof was restored in 1910 as the tower had been used as a vicarage until the early seventeenth century.

The tower has a vaulted basement where cattle and livestock would have been sheltered during raids. The priest would have lived on the top two floors, however the absence of windows on some walls show it has been built for defence.

Today it is a grade 1 listed building and houses a collection of medieval stone artefacts.

Dunstanburgh Castle
"Lancaster's Jewel in the North"

At eleven acres (4.5 Hectares) Dunstanburgh covers the largest area of any of the Northumberland castles. It stands on a lonely yet majestic outcrop of basalt on the shore of the North Sea near the Northumberland village of Craster. We can imagine the Castle in its heyday, full of imposing strength, withstanding both its enemies and the storms washing in from the inhospitable North Sea.

Building on the Castle started in 1313 under the instruction of Thomas Earl of Lancaster, cousin of King Edward II of England and arch critic of the King. Licence to crenellate was granted to Thomas in 1316, before they fell out and Thomas had sided with the barons in open revolt of the King. The Castle was built to show the stature and the strength of Thomas and consequently has a very high standard of masonry. He was also a romantic and envisaged a castle like Camelot on the coast. By the time the Castle was almost finished around 1322, Thomas had been defeated at the Battle of Boroughbridge and executed. On his death his lands, including the Castle were forfeited. In 1323 his younger brother petitioned successfully for the restoration of Thomas's estate to himself.

The great moat of the Castle was completed by Michaelmas around September, 1314. Measuring eighty feet wide and eighteen feet deep it would have taken an immense amount of manpower to dig this, while at the same time construct the gatehouse. In 1323 John de Lilburn the constable of Dunstanburgh at that time had the three-storey Lilburn Tower constructed on the north-west side of the Castle. A thirty feet square tower with walls that are six feet thick.

The Constables tower and bakehouse within the Castle walls.

To the east of the great gatehouse and built onto the curtain wall is the Constable Tower, the residence of the constable or keeper of the Castle. Inside the inner ward in front of Constable's Tower are the remains of the bakehouse and other buildings used to service the castle.

Later in the fourteenth century the Castle passed to John of Gaunt, who extensively renovated and modified it, making the formidable south-facing gatehouse into a keep to house himself and his retinue.

He blocked up the gateway, and made that into a magnificent three-storey Don Jon (keep), building a new entrance on the north-western curtain wall. It is thought that there was a small harbour in the rocks to the south east of the Castle in front of Queen Margaret's or Egynclugh Tower so that it could be supplied from the sea, as in some of the great castles of North Wales, although there is no evidence that it was styled on any of them. The port and harbour lasted until the reign of Henry VIII as some of his fleet used it to shelter from a storm.

The Main Gatehouse of Dunstanburgh Castle added by John of Gaunt

In the War of the Roses Dunstanburgh sided with the Lancastrian cause. It did however change hands a number of times and finally surrendered in 1464, just before the surrender of Bamburgh and Alnwick. By 1550 the Castle was finished as a fortress. The damage had been done and Dunstanburgh didn't recover, to this day it stands as a magnificent ruin and tribute to its heyday. Today it is cared for by English Heritage and can be seen by all.

Edlingham Castle

Nestling about five miles west of Alnwick in the northern Northumberland countryside is Edlingham, a small village with an eleventh-century church and the ruins of a castle. The Castle was originally a manor house built in the mid thirteenth century by John de Edlingham. This wasn't fortified and contained two floors. At the time of its construction there was no need for the defences, as the borders and that area of Northumberland were both a peaceful and prosperous area.

All this changed in 1296 when Edward I of England cast his envious eye at Scotland. At around the same time the castle changed hands when Sir William de Felton, a sherriff of Northumberland, acquired it. With the Anglo-Scottish war the need to fortify the manor was imperative. To this end a stone palisade was built. The palisade also included a moat (unfortunately there is no trace of this now) and a stone gatehouse, as the entrance into what had become the courtyard.

In around 1340 the solar tower was built, thus strengthening the Castle further and improving the living accommodation for the inhabitants with well-appointed rooms.

At around 1400 the manor started to be referred to as a castle, this would assume that the De Feltons or Hastings had received a licence to crenellate from the King.

The ownership of the Castle passed to the Hastings family in the early fifteenth century, probably around 1402. The families concentrated on farming but the Castle was necessary to protect livestock from what were the raids of the reivers from Scotland and other parts of Northumberland. In the early part of the sixteenth century the Castle was acquired by the Swinburnes, but by about the 1650s the Castle had fallen into disrepair.

Today the ruins are in the custody of English Heritage who have cared for the site since 1978.

Edlingham Tower

Situated not far from the castle at Edlingham is the beautiful church of St John the Baptist. There has been a church on this site since the eigth century when the lands were given to St Cuthbert and the monks of Lindisfarne Abbey by King Ceolwulf of Northumbria

The present church was built in the late eleventh century. It contains a rare Norman tunnel vault and attached to the west of the church is a pele tower which probably dates from the twelfth century, it was used as a defensive tower for the priests during the sixteenth century, as raids from both Scotland and other parts of the north were common during this period.

The Tower is a strong square format adorned with arrow-slit windows to keep the raiders at bay and give sanctuary to the priest and the locals. The Tower would have been built probably before the Castle was fortified and crenellated. It is not unlike many of the vicars pele towers in this part of Northumberland, but Edlingham is probably one of the oldest.

Embleton Vicars Pele

Just inland from the beautiful north Northumberland coast is the village of Embleton and its church, Holy Trinity, dating from the twelfth century in its earliest parts. Alongside the vicarage, a few yards to the south of the church, is the fourteenth-century pele tower which gave sanctuary and safety to the priest during troubled times.

The tower was built in 1395 in response to repeated Scottish raids on the village. The tower was built by Merton College, Oxford, which held the patronage of the village in the fourteenth century. One of the first things that strikes you with this building is its size, in relation to comparable vicars pele towers built around this time, is that it's much bigger, being three storeys high and much wider. Even being attached to the later nineteenth-century-built vicarage the size is immediately apparent.

The tower today is a grade II listed building, in need of some care and restoration along with the vicarage.

Etal Castle
"To the Manners Born"

Standing at the end of the main street in the picturesque village of Etal lies this fourteenth-century castle. The Castle was built under the instruction of Robert de Manners in order to protect his family and lands from cross-border raids and his continuing dispute with the Heron family of nearby Ford Castle. This feud with the Herons, whist lasting a considerable amount of time, wasn't as bloody nor did it end in the battle that the Maxwell Johnstone feud did across the Border in Scotland.

The Castle has two main towers. One is the gatehouse facing the village, the other is the keep within the inner ward. The keep or tower house is within the inner ward and is a three-storey construction, giving living accommodation for the family on the first floor and their servants. When originally built the house wouldn't be fortified, the licence to crenellate was granted to Sir Robert Manners in 1341. The house was then transformed into the fortified tower with the gatehouse and walls.

The gatehouse served both as a guard room and on its first floor as a chapel, indicated by the ornate window facing out into the inner ward. The portcullis (the one seen today is a modern copy) and the drawbridge winch was housed in the gatehouse towers. This would have been the main entrance to the Castle during medieval times. The gatehouse is attached to the south curtain wall, the only piece of external wall still standing. This curtain wall also connects to the remains of the south-west tower, which is the Castle entrance today.

Prior to the fourteenth century the manor of Etal was a tenancy from the barony of Wooler. The Manners family acquired it in or around 1180 when they would construct a manor house; this would no doubt be a timber-framed building. However post 1296 and the Scottish wars of independence, Etal's very close proximity to the Scottish Border would mean that they would then build a stone manor house and ask for the licence to crenellate in order to protect themselves.

Robert died in 1354 and was succeeded by his son John who continued to build and fortify the Castle, indeed he probably did most to make the Castle look like it does today. A survey in 1368 is the first time that Etal is referred to as a castle. John was succeeded by first his son Robert, who married well and added considerable lands to the family's holdings, then his son Robert who, it is thought, was the instigator of the disputes with their neighbours at Ford, the Heron family. The feud ended in 1438, but it was financially ruinous for the Manners family with their worth depreciating over this period.

Robert Manners was granted a knighthood for his services to Sir Henry Percy in looking after the borders. He was killed at the Battle of Towton, fighting for the Lancastrian cause, in the War of the Roses, whilst serving the Percy family. Sir Henry Percy also fell at the same battle.

Sir Robert's son also called Robert succeeded him, again serving on the Scottish Border. Robert was succeeded by his son George, who married the niece of Henry IV adding considerable lands to the family's estates, but this meant that the Castle was abandoned as a primary residence and it was left in the hands of a constable.

At the start of the sixteenth century the constable was John Collingwood. It was during his time, when in 1513 King James IV of Scotland marched south with an army of 30,000 and a considerable amount of ordinance. Etal fell to the Scots after a short siege as it was decided by Collingwood that the Castle wouldn't take sustained attack from cannon fire of the type brought south by the Scots. The battle was disastrous for the Scots and afterwards the captured guns were brought to Etal for safekeeping. You can see where the stone has been removed and replaced at the base of the keep to facilitate the storage of the guns after the battle.

By 1564 when the Earl of Winchester visited the Castle it was already in a state of disrepair, this would continue until after the Union of the Crowns in 1603. With the union of the crowns, castles like Etal weren't needed and the Castle fell into neglect. The Castle and its lands were first sold to Baron Hume of Berwick, then to Lord Howard the Earl of Suffolk, and then to Robert Carr who was related to the Heron of Ford. Robert held the Castle for Charles I during the Civil War. After the defeat of Charles his lands were forfeit. These were returned to the family when the Stuart dynasty was returned to the throne.

Today the Castle is cared for by English Heritage.

Ford Castle

Situated in northern Northumberland on the banks of the River Till, a tributary of the River Tweed, Ford Castle is probably best known for the dalliance of James IV of Scotland with Lady Heron, a noted beauty, on the eve of the Battle of Flodden Field in 1513.

The manor house at Ford was built in the thirteenth century by Odinel de Forde, after whom the Castle and village are named. The licence to crenellate was given in 1338 by Edward III at a time when the threat from Scotland was looming large. After their success at Bannockburn the Scots had laid waste to large areas of Northumberland. By this time the Castle or manor had passed to Sir William Heron, a supporter of Edward III. Sir William had served as Sherriff of Bamburgh, Pickering and Scarborough castles as well as High Sherriff of Northumberland.

In 1385 the Scots captured the Castle, starting a turbulent period in the Castle's history. Sir William was imprisoned in 1388 in Newcastle, but later released and rebuilt Ford after its capture by the Scots. Sir Henry Lilburn raided the Castle and murdered the entire garrison there in 1388; this was a raid from the English side of the Border proving that enemies were on both sides of the Border.

The entrance to Ford Castle, with King James's tower behind.

In 1415 the Castle is mentioned in a list of fortifications in Northumberland, however in 1430 it is listed as being in poor repair. It must have been later repaired as it was held by the Scots on their way to Flodden, giving rise to the popular tale of the dalliance with Lady Heron. Sadly the tale is a myth, although she did try to get King James to spare the Castle in exchange for the release of two Scottish knights. The Earl of Surrey agreed to this exchange; however the Scots burnt the Castle regardless. In a survey carried out for Henry VIII in 1541, the Castle was still not fully repaired.

In 1549 the Castle passed from the Heron family to the Carr family by marriage. Indeed a romantic tale of the marriage surrounds young Thomas Carr, who defended the Castle from one of the towers against a French-led Scottish army in 1549. He held out in what is known as King James's Tower. The Castle had been battered by cannon until young Tom was left, defending the tower, which he did so gallantly the young heiress was so smitten with the bold defender that they were married. Some of the Heron family wished to take the Castle back and set out for the Castle with this in mind, however word reached Thomas Carr and the raiders were attacked on their way to the Castle and defeated.

A hundred years later the Castle was to change hands again by marriage, this time to Sir Francis Blake of Cogges in Oxfordshire. Sir Francis set about building a mansion in the grounds of the Castle, with building starting around 1694. When Sir Francis died in 1717 having been predeceased by his daughter Mary, the Castle passed to his daughter's husband.

Passing down the generations of the Blake family, the Castle and hall next came into the ownership of the Marquis of Waterford, who had married Susannah the heiress and granddaughter of Francis Blake. At this point the hall was substantially remodelled.

In 1907 it was acquired by the Joicey family, who then leased it to Northumberland County Council as a young person's residential care centre. Today it is an outward-bound centre.

Lindisfarne Castle
"The Guardian of the Holy Isle"

This Castle is situated on the top of the basalt rock at the entrance to the natural harbour of Lindisfarne, "the Holy Isle". It is a magnificent vision to all visitors both from the sea and over the causeway to the Island. Logic would indicate that the Castle was built to protect the monastery on Lindisfarne. Unfortunately this isn't true, as there may well have been a castle on the rock before the dissolution of the monasteries started in 1530, and the Castle wasn't built or at least started until 1539 on the orders of King Henry VIII.

Henry's idea was that the Castle would protect the small natural harbour on the Island. However Henry, who died in 1547, would not live to see the Castle complete and garrisoned, the first soldiers arriving by boat in 1550. The monastery on Lindisfarne had to all effect ceased to function when Robert Rooke of Berwick undertook to build the Castle. He didn't have to worry about a supply of stone as the old monastery provided it in abundance. It is unlikely that the major raid into Scotland that Henry planned to launch from the Castle ever took place.

After the Union of the Crowns in 1603, the Castle had little military value as the threat from Scotland had gone. There remained a garrison there, but on a much smaller scale than in Tudor times. The Castle didn't even see action during the Civil War, although it was visited by a Royalist who remarked how good the Castle was.

During the Jacobite rebellion of 1715 the Castle didn't see any action. It was only garrisoned by one gunner, who doubled up as the local barber. The barber/gunner had a visit from a Lancelot Errington, a known Jacobite sympathiser. After receiving his haircut Errington went away and returned later in the company of his nephew. They had the gunner open up the Castle, after holding a pistol to his head. The barber/gunner left. Leaving the Castle in the hands of Errington and his nephew, they held it for only a few days. They expected reinforcements but, to their dismay, these never came. Instead they were captured and thrown in Berwick gaol. This would normally have been the end, however our intrepid duo tunnelled their way out and made their way to Bamburgh, where they hid for a few days avoiding recapture. They then escaped completely, not to be seen in those parts again.

During the latter part of the nineteenth century and the beginning of the twentieth century, the Castle served as a coastguard station. The castle was bought around this time by a Mr Edward Hudson, the creator of *Country Life* Magazine. He employed his friend, the eminent architect Sir Edwin Lutyens, to convert the Castle into a private residence, this incorporated sash windows and period furniture.

Today the Castle is in the careful hands of the National Trust and is open to the general public.

Naworth Castle

The beautiful Naworth Castle is situated two miles from the village of Brampton in Cumbria and about the same distance from the historic Lanercost Priory. It is inextricably linked to two families who have had a prominent place in the history of the English western march. The Dacres and later, through marriage, the Howards, both also linked with one of the most famous battles in the borders, Flodden Field.

The lands in the area were originally held by the ancient earls of Northumberland, however Ranulf de Dacre was given permission to crenellate his manor at Naworth in 1335, by Edward III. Edward was no stranger to giving permission to his lords to crenellate, in particular those in the borders, in order to strengthen his hold on this area from the Scots and also to keep his barons happy. The tower that Ranulf de Dacre built was in effect a pele tower, known today as the Dacre Tower and is the oldest part of the Castle. The tower then had a courtyard and was enclosed by an outer wall.

After Ranulf's death the Dacres preferred to use their residence at Irthington as their primary residence. This unfortunately meant that Naworth fell into disrepair. This carried on for almost two centuries until the barony was inherited by

Lord Thomas Dacre, who had the vision to see that Naworth was worth using as a residence and developing. He used Naworth during his time as Warden of the Western March. He greatly strengthened the Castle against the Scots and for that matter the considerable number of reivers in the area.

Lord Thomas Dacre was a renowned military leader and fearless in battle. It was he who commanded the reserve at the battle of Flodden for Thomas Howard, the Earl of Surrey and he recognised King James IV's body after the battle. For this service Henry VIII made Dacre a Knight of the Garter. Lord Thomas added the Great Hall and what is now known as William Howard's Tower to the Castle. After his death the Castle, in all its majesty, fell once again into neglect until William Howard obtained it.

Lord William Howard was the third son of the Duke of Norfolk, no stranger to the Dacres. Indeed Lord William had married the heiress Elizabeth Dacre. Elizabeth had inherited the barony of Gilsland and with it Naworth, by this time in some considerable state of disrepair. Lord William, like Lord Thomas before him, had vision and this vision included grand ideas for Naworth. Whilst they married young, William was fifteen and Elizabeth was fourteen, it was by all accounts a very happy marriage and a very long one producing ten sons and five daughters.

They arrived at Naworth later in life and set about restoring the Castle. This work was carried out at the start of the seventeenth century. The Jacobean period was in full swing and this was the décor they chose for the Castle, a look it retains to this day. Unfortunately in 1844 the Castle was almost destroyed by fire. Yet it did survive and prosper with the Morpeth Tower being constructed after the fire.

Today Naworth is a private residence and not open to the public, however it does hold corporate functions.

Norham Castle
"Castle of the Prince Bishops"

Standing high above the River Tweed on the English side of the Border, defended on its northern and western flanks by the river and steep cliffs, this Castle proudly stands guard on the Border looking out for the danger that was always threatened from the north. The original Castle was built around the early part of the twelfth century by Ranulf Flambard, Bishop of Durham, At that time the Castle and the lands of Norhamshire were under the control of the Bishopric of Durham. It was indeed a border stronghold and would play its part in the turbulent border history.

When civil war broke out in 1135 between Stephen and Matilda, more commonly called "The Anarchy", the Castle was strengthened as King David of Scotland invaded Northumberland to lay claim to the lands around whilst the war raged in the south of England. So later in 1136 Norham was besieged by Scots for the first time, this would be a regular occurrence over the next 500 years.

David I invaded Northumberland again in 1138 and Norham was once again besieged when he laid waste to a lot of the county before being defeated by Thurston, Bishop of York in "the Battle of the Standard" near Northallerton. However even in this defeat David I still retained Northumberland for Scotland. They were given back to England by Malcolm IV to Henry II. Only when the Treaty of York was signed on 25 September 1237 between Henry III of England and Alexander II of Scotland did the Scots give up their claims on Northumberland. This defined the eastern part of the Border as the River Tweed and the Cheviot Hills.

Throughout this time the Castle at Norham stayed under the control of the Bishopric of Durham. The Castle had been substantially destroyed by David in 1138 but was rebuilt on the orders of Henry II (who also built the main keep at Newcastle). This was under the guidance of Hugh de Puiset, the incumbent Bishop of Durham, and Hugh also built the chancel at Norham Church. Hugh's rebuilding included the Great Tower.

Under the reign of King John the Castle was expanded to have the outer ward where previously only the inner wards had been constructed. This rebuilding was probably done in stone rather than the wooden construction previously used, and as such forms the oldest parts of what we see today. Standing five storeys the central keep is indeed an impressive grand tower. At this time the castle at Berwick was held by the Scots, having been sold to them in 1199, by Richard I to fund the Third Crusade; this made Norham strategically important to the English.

Besieged again in 1215, for forty days by Alexander II, son of William the Lion. The siege was unsuccessful and the Castle held out. Peace was restored when the Treaty of Birgham was signed at Norham in 1219. This treaty and the Treaty of York ensured there was peace in the borders until the end of the thirteenth century. This peace was shattered in 1291 when, after the death of Alexander III of Scotland, Edward I of England was asked to arbitrate on who should be the next King of Scotland, there were thirteen candidates in what became known as "the Great Cause". Edward was entertained for this at Norham by the Bishop of Durham, Anthony Beck. Edward stayed for a year before declaring for John Balliol on provision that he paid homage to him as overlord of Scotland, which was duly done in Norham Church.

This culminated in the Scottish Wars of Independence, and ended at first with the death of Edward I and then the subsequent defeat of his son Edward II at Bannockburn. In between Robert the Bruce invaded Northumberland in 1311 and again a year later. However Norham being at that time well fortified was avoided in favour of easier targets. This led to nearly 300 years of border warfare and raiding.

The Castle was significantly remodelled and rebuilt in the early fifteenth century; this concerned the west or main gate and modifying the Great Tower as well as building a new tower. The Castle only figured briefly in the Wars of the Roses with other castles in Northumberland, Alnwick, Bamburgh and Dunstanburgh all being held for the Lancastrian cause. Norham surrendered to the Earl of Warwick in 1464, the same year as Bamburgh and Dunstanburgh fell.

In 1497 the Castle was besieged again by a Scottish army, led by James IV and Perkin Warbeck, the Pretender to the English throne. This time the Castle came under cannon fire from the renowned canon 'Mons Meg', the great gun making short work of the outer ward. This led to strengthening of the defences to withstand cannon. The Castle underwent further rebuilding after this, finishing in the early sixteenth century.

In 1513 when James IV set out to invade England again, whilst his uncle Henry VIII was away fighting in France, Norham was again under Scottish siege, this time with even more ordinance. The bronze cannons had been brought down from Linlithgow. The outer ward fell within two days of the onslaught and the Castle was taken. Following the Scots' defeat at Flodden a few days later, the Castle was returned to the Bishop of Durham. Further repairs were made and the construction of Clapham's Tower commenced (Clapham was the captain of the Castle at that time). In 1523 Thomas Howard, Earl of Surrey, moved cannon from Portsmouth to bolster the defences at Norham.

In 1559 the then Bishop of Durham, Bishop Tunstall refused to take the Oath of Supremacy to Elizabeth I, so the Castle and the surrounding area of Norhamshire was forfeited to the Crown. It would appear from records that from this point on the Castle had little money spent on it, and whilst garrisoned throughout the sixteenth century it fell further and further into decay. By the early seventeenth century and the Union of the Crowns the Castle was no longer needed and was never used even during the Civil War. Today, the Castle is looked after English Heritage.

Penrith Castle
"A Castle fit for Kings"

Penrith Castle was thought to have been started by William Strickland who would later become the Bishop of Carlisle, in 1399. However it is now thought that this Castle was built by Ralph Neville of the strong Neville family who also held Raby Castle in County Durham in the latter stages of the fourteenth century or early fifteenth. He had been granted the manor of Penrith in 1396, at that time the town of Penrith although much smaller than the current town was subject to frequent raids from the Scottish side of the border. The purpose of the Castle was to protect the town and the Nevilles' assets in that area and, in his capacity as warden of the English West March, the head of the Neville family's responsibility for the defence of the western side of the Border.

Ralph Neville's son Richard Earl of Warwick, known as Warwick the Kingmaker, inherited the Castle and further developed the buildings, adding the Red Tower and the great hall.

On the death of Richard Neville in 1471 the Castle passed to another Richard, this time the Duke of Gloucester who would later become King Richard III, who served time as the Warden of the West March. This then made the Castle Crown property, where it would remain until the reign of King William III (William of Orange).

Further modifications were carried out at this time, including raising the curtain wall, so that buildings with larger windows could be built on the inside of the Castle. This also included a bakery and a brewery. After Richard was crowned, the Castle ceased to be a permanent residence for him, as he spent more time in London. In all probability this was the high point of the history of the Castle.

To all intents and purposes a hundred years later it had been all but abandoned and some of the stone had been taken to construct a prison. Queen Elizabeth instructed Lord Thomas Scrope to check if the Castle could be put into a defensible state to guard against renewed Scottish raids. He informed her that it would take some £300 to make the Castle serviceable again; needless to say, prudence of the royal coffers prevailed and the work was not carried out.

The Castle was briefly occupied during the Civil War by Parliamentarian forces under the command of Major-General Lambert. His men, some 300 of them, were garrisoned in the town; the last time the Castle was used in any capacity.

Today some of the Red Tower still stands, and in parts some of the curtain wall. Enough remains of the Castle to get an idea of its strength and past glory. The Castle is situated opposite the railway station on a small mound in Castle Park and is easily accessible.

Preston Tower
"Half a Castle"

Just south of Ellingham and about a mile to the east of the A1 are the remains of Preston Tower. This was constructed around 1390 and built by Sir Robert Harbottle, who was in the service of the constable of Berwick. Around the time of the Tower's construction Sir Robert was said to have committed murder, a crime he was subsequently pardoned for.

Sir Robert married Isobel, the daughter and heiress of Sir Bertram Monboucher of Horton, in 1399. Well thought of by Henry IV, who made him sherriff after the Battle of Otterburn, and then Constable of Dunstanburgh Castle a few miles to the south-west on the Northumberland coast. The Tower itself is first mentioned in a listing of one of seventy-eight similar towers in Northumberland, which was known as the "List of Fortalices".

The Tower originally had four turrets, one at each corner so it would have been double the size we see today as only two of the turrets remain. The other two turrets were demolished in 1603 at the Union of the Crowns. The small arrow-slit windows show its primary function was the defence and protection of its occupants. The windows now have glass in them, which then would have been too expensive and the windows would have been shuttered.

The Tower would have had to stand constant reivers raids during the sixteenth century, as these would be frequent during the winter months as the borders were in an almost constant state of war, in contrast to the south of England that was in what could be termed peace.

Sir Gulschard Harbottle fought for Henry VIII with the Earl of Surrey at the Battle of Flodden. The Tower then passed to his daughter as there was no male heir. She married Sir Thomas Percy the 6th Earl of Northumberland. Their son Thomas, who became the 7th Earl, was beheaded at York in 1572 for his part in "the Rising of the Northern Earls" in 1569. The Tower was then confiscated for the Crown. From then the Tower was leased or sold to various people until it was purchased by A.J. Baker Cresswell in 1861. It is still in the owned and cared for by the Baker Cresswell family.

Prudhoe Castle
"Never Taken by the Scots"

Almost hidden by trees and on top of a rocky plateau above the River Tyne stands Prudhoe Castle. Today it is a peaceful scene with the millpond to the left as you approach the gatehouse and entrance to the Castle.

The barony of Prudhoe dates back to before the time of William the Conqueror and in all probability was a Saxon manor. The lands around, and the barony were granted to the Norman knight Robert d'Umfraville in 1080 in order to effect law and order in the area which also included the barony of Redesdale.

For the next 150 years Northumberland was disputed territory between the English and Scottish crowns, so much so that in 1139 the earldom of Northumberland was granted to the Scottish King in order to pacify the claims. This resulted in the Northumbrian barons and their Scottish counterparts mixing freely at the Scottish court and cross-border marriages weren't uncommon.

The d'Umfravilles, indeed were often at the Scottish court and Odinel d'Umfraville spent a considerable amount of time there together with the future Scottish King, William the Lion. Henry II reclaimed the earldom of Northumberland for the English in 1154, infuriating the Scottish King William the Lion. Despite knowing William well, Odinel sided with the English King, Henry. William invaded Northumberland in 1173 and besieged Prudhoe, and again in 1174. Following this second attempt William was captured after a battle near Alnwick, along with some of his Flemish guard. Odinel was rewarded for this by permission being granted to rebuild the Castle at Prudhoe in stone.

Prudhoe gatehouse from the inner ward

During the thirteenth century the Umfraville wealth and standing increased significantly. The marriage of Gilbert Umfraville, descendent of Odinel by Matilda, who was heir to the earldom of Angus, keeping the Earl of Angus title in the family until 1314, when Robert D'Umfraville lost the title after the Battle of Bannockburn. By the end of the thirteenth century Edward I had led his army into Scotland starting the first Scottish War of Independence. The northern counties were divided into three marches, Prudhoe then came under the English Middle March controlled from Alnwick Castle and it was probably the first time the Percys had come into contact with the manor of Prudhoe.

During the fourteenth century the Percy family became ever more powerful in the north. Originally settling in North Yorkshire their influence became more and more felt in Northumberland. Becoming the Earls of Northumberland under Richard II, with the title granted to Henry Percy. Henry married the widow of Gilbert Umfraville, Matilda Lucy, thus gaining the Barony of Prudhoe and half of his lands. Gilbert's lands in Redesdale going to another branch of the Umfraville

Inside the main hall at Prudhoe Castle

family. Prudhoe was then controlled from Alnwick, the main base for the Percy family.

At the beginning of the fifteenth century Henry and his son Harry, the famous Hotspur, rebelled in collusion with Owain Glyndwr against Henry IV, this rebellion culminated in the death of Hotspur in the Battle of Shrewsbury in 1403. Percy lands were then confiscated and given to Henry's brother John, the Duke of Lancaster. The Barony passed back to the Percys in 1470. During the War of the Roses Prudhoe was captured by Edward IV for the Yorkist cause.

Under the Tudors Prudhoe was largely forgotten and remained unaltered. Sir Henry Percy the 6th Earl deciding to use Prudhoe as a residence while Warden of the Middle March. His brother Sir Thomas Percy used the Castle after the Pilgrimage of Grace in 1536. The 7th Earl Sir Thomas, also known as simple Tom, rebelled against Elizabeth I in the Rising of the Northern Earls in 1569. After Sir Tom was executed at York in 1572 the Percy's were forbidden to live in the north but kept their lands. By 1590 and the 9th Earl, Prudhoe was in a state of disrepair, with not enough income from the surrounding lands.

The revival of Prudhoe began in 1835 with the coming of the railway to the Tyne valley. The Castle then had a variety of uses, officers of the Northumberland Fusiliers used the Manor House Flats and then a Spanish consul used them. In 1966 the Castle came under state guardianship, though still being owned by the Percy family, the Dukes of Northumberland. Today the Castle is in the care of English Heritage.

Thirlwall Castle
"Nicely Tucked Away"

Tucked away in the south-west corner of Northumberland and just outside the village of Greenhead, high above the Tipalt burn is Thirlwall Castle. The name Thirlwall is from old English meaning a gap in the wall. Today it's only a silent ruin of power in days gone by, but a quiet spot to contemplate history. The Castle is on a mound with the burn below and, even though there are other hillocks nearby that are taller and which would have given a better vantage point to warn of raiders, we can only imagine that the proximity to the burn played a key part in the siting of the Castle.

Built sometime around 1255 almost entirely from stone taken from Hadrian's Wall which is close by. At the time of its building by the Thirlwall family Northumberland was under Scottish control. The Castle is almost square and in 1541 it was in good repair, being used to repel reivers from the north.

The Castle was built by the Thirlwall family who by all accounts were quite warlike, obviously men of their time with the cry "A Thirlwall! A Thirlwall!" as they went into battle. The first recorded incident of the Thirlwalls is when the local Prioress of Lambley Priory grazed her cattle on Thirlwall land and was challenged. Her response to this was to challenge Baron Thirlwall to combat to solve the dispute – quite a common occurrence to settle disputes in the 14th century. It would take some formidable prioress to do this; however she would, in most probability, have used a champion of her own to make the challenge. The challenge however never came to pass with the prioress paying £10 in settlement and a further £20 after having someone, thought to be a shepherd, set fire to a hut on Baron Thirlwall's land.

The warlike Thirlwalls battled at Falkirk against William Wallace. Sir John de Thirlwall was actually laid low by Wallace with an axe while holding a pele tower, surviving that escapade he lived to the ripe old age of eighty-five, no mean feat in troubled times.

The Castle fell into disrepair in the early seventeenth century when the reiving times were all but over due to the Union of the Crowns. The Castle was sold in 1748 to the Howards of Naworth in Cumbria for £4,000. However, they only required the land attached to the barony and let the Castle fall into ruins, never to be used in anger again.

Twizel Castle
"Above the Bridge"

High above the River Till and overlooking the medieval bridge built in 1511 that both the English and Scottish armies crossed on their way to the fateful battle at Flodden, lies Twizel Castle. The castle ruins that we see today are from a structure started in 1770 and not the pele tower that was in existence at the time of the Battle of Flodden in 1513.

The original tower on this site was built in the fifteenth century probably around 1415 by the Heron family, some of whom owned nearby Ford Castle. In 1496 the tower was burnt by Perkin Warbeck, pretender to the English throne and James IV in one of their many raids into Northumberland. There is no mention of what happened to Twizel's tower when James IV invaded England again in 1513, culminating in the Battle of Flodden.

In 1520 the Heron family sold it to another well-known Northumberland family, the Selbys. The tower was attacked again around 1546, but survived. A survey in 1561 said that the tower and the outer barmkin wall were still standing although it wasn't known whether it was inhabited. The tower lasted until after the Union of the Crowns in 1603, when little is recorded about its state.

Sir Francis Blake had grand plans from 1770 to build a six-story manor house on the same spot as the original tower, so the tower was demolished to make way for the proposed manor. However Sir Francis died before completion and his son took over the building of the house. His plans were grander than his father's and the money, sadly, ran out before the completion of the house. This, together with his electioneering drove the younger Sir Francis to ruin and into a debtors' sanctuary in Holyrood Abbey.

Today, unfortunately, the Castle lies derelict and overgrown. It is looked after by Tillmouth Estates.

Warkworth Castle
"The Lion of the North"

Standing high above a loop in the beautiful River Coquet, Warkworth Castle stands proud as a guardian of England's northern Border. It is a fabulous location for a wonderful fortress. It sits on a rock with views over the village of Warkworth and out to the North Sea. The Castle is an imposing structure with large towers and a magnificent donjon or keep.

It has its origins in the middle of the twelfth century, when the manor of Warkworth was granted to Roger Fitz Eustace by Henry II, himself no mean castle builder, and he also retained an interest in Bamburgh and Newcastle where he ordered the construction of the great keep. It is more than likely that there was a fortification of some description prior to the building of the Castle we see, today.

Previously it was thought the Castle had been held by Henry, son of David I of Scotland under the Treaty of Durham, when

Henry became Earl of Northumberland. This, though, is not substantiated in fact, in what documentation is left from the time, but Henry did however hold Bamburgh. In all likelihood Henry II had the Castle built along with Newcastle when he took repossession of Northumberland in around 1150. In 1173 when William the Lion of Scotland invaded Northumberland, Warkworth was abandoned in favour of Newcastle as the defences there were more substantial, whereas Warkworth defences were deemed feeble. This resulted in the Earl of Fife attacking the Castle and putting all to the sword, including those who had sought refuge in the local church.

The Fitz Eustace family also had great lands in East Anglia, where Roger's son Robert resided in 1178, when Roger died. However Robert increasingly spent more time in Northumberland. King John made him Sheriff of Northumberland in 1203; he built large parts of the Castle and indeed entertained King John here in 1213 a year before Rogers's death.

With the ascension to the throne of Edward I, the attention of the English crown looked north towards Scotland. The Northumberland castles and Warkworth would play their part. At this time the Castle was held by Robert Fitz Eustace, grandson of the first Robert. Robert was captured at the English defeat in the Battle of Stirling Bridge in 1297. The Castle was then run by a constable for a period of time but there appears to have been a dispute over money around this time which later had repercussions. So much so that when Robert's son John de Clavering took over the Castle in 1310, he was forced to hand over the Castle to the Crown in settlement of death duties. After the defeat at Bannockburn it was by royal command that Warkworth be strengthened and the King also partly garrisoned the Castle to ward against increased Scottish raids.

When John de Clavering died in 1332, Edward III granted the Castle to Henry de Percy, he had actually done this in 1328 even though John de Clavering still occupied the Castle. It was a royal castle at the time. Thus began the association with the Percy family that would last until the present day.

The first Earl of Northumberland, Henry Percy, is less well known than his more famous son Henry, or Harry Hotspur as he is more often referred to. However both father and son were involved in a conspiracy with Owain Glyndwr against Henry IV culminating in the Battle of Shrewsbury in 1403, during which Hotspur was slain and the rebellion defeated. The Percy estates were then forfeited to the Crown including Warkworth. The lands and title were restored to Henry's son in an act of royal clemency and he became 2nd Earl of Northumberland, and later Warden of the Eastern Marches on the English side. The young Percy rebelled against King Henry IV in 1405. The King marched quickly north, but Percy fled to Scotland and, after a short defence, the Castle surrendered to Henry.

The Castle was then given to John of Lancaster one of Henry's sons. On the ascension of Henry V in 1413, the Castle was restored to the Percy family, indeed to the son of Harry Hotspur also called Henry. He became the second Earl; he died in 1455 fighting for the Lancastrian cause in the Wars of the Roses. Succeeded by another Henry as the 3rd Earl, he suffered a similar fate, being killed in the Battle of Towton. The son of the 3rd Earl inherited the title in 1471, succeeded by the 4th Earl who refused to commit at the Battle of Bosworth in 1485. He was later murdered, in 1489.

With the Tudor Henry VII on the throne of England a new chapter began for Warkworth and the Percys. The 5th Earl maintained the buildings at Warkworth; this was also carried on by the 6th Earl. The 6th Earl Henry Percy died without issue in 1537. His brother Thomas Percy had been executed the previous year 1536 for his part in the Pilgrimage of Grace. The family and his descendants inherited the Castle in 1557 when Queen Mary I gave the lands and titles back. Unfortunately the Castle had not been maintained and was in a state of disrepair.

The 7th Earl Thomas Percy took part in the unsuccessful Rising of the Northern Earls in 1569. Warkworth was initially held by servants loyal to the Earl, but it was later taken and occupied by Lord Hunsdon for the Crown and Queen Elizabeth. Percy was executed at York in 1572. In 1574 Elizabeth granted the lands and titles back to the 7th Earl's son.

The Percy's did not learn and with the ascension of the Stuarts and James VI to the throne of England the 9th Earl was arrested following the Gunpowder Plot. He was fined an enormous sum of £30,000 and sent to the Tower of London and Warkworth was leased to Sir Ralph Gray of Chillingham, who entertained James I there in 1617.

During the Civil War the Castle was garrisoned for the Royalists but surrendered to a Scottish army in 1644. The 10th Earl tried to get redress for the damage done by Parliamentarian forces in 1649. This started the downward spiral of the Castle. Nothing would happen with the Castle for over 100 years until the Percy family were elevated to Dukes of Northumberland. The 4th Duke started the rebuilding of the keep or great tower. He used these rooms and members of the family did until well into the twentieth century. The Castle was handed over to the Crown for keeping and today it is looked after by English Heritage, so we can all share this magnificent ruin.

Woodhouses Bastle
"The Strong Pele"

Lying on a hillside, not far from the little village of Hepple and just off the Holystone Road in upper Coquetdale, is Woodhouses Bastle house, a fortified farmhouse dating from the sixteenth century. Although the lintel above the door would have us believe that it was built in 1602 it is actually older than this, one of numerous bastle houses on the both sides of the Border.

It is thought that it was built for the Potte family around 1540 as it is mentioned in a survey of 1541 when it is referred to as a "Very Strong Pele". The house is complete, with a smaller ruined structure beside it. It has a very small entrance to one side and the stairs on this bastle house are internal and no entrance can be seen on the first floor from the outside. There are arrow-slit windows in the ends for the defence of the house. The house would be built for protection from the raids that would have come from Redesdale as well as Tynedale and Scotland.

The lower floor has a vaulted (arched) ceiling in keeping with the design so common during the sixteenth century. The wooden door, which is now missing, would have been protected by a second outer iron door called a yet: this further strengthened the defence of the bastle.

Other English Fortifications

Askerton Castle

Forming part of a farm today on the outskirts of Askerton in Cumbria, the grade 1 listed building was built for Lord Thomas Dacre, the 2nd Baron Dacre of Gilsland. Originally built as a manor house it was fortified later as the troubles along the Border increased, and indeed the raids from the Armstrongs and Elliots in the Debateable Lands were frequent. The Dacres fortified the house whilst they held the position of Warden of the West March. Later in the sixteenth century The castle was owned by Thomas Carleton, the land sergeant of Gilsland and an associate of Richie Graham of Brackenhill. Today Askerton is a private residence and not open to the public.

Beadnell Tower

In the village of Beadnell just south of Seahouses in Northumberland is situated Beadnell Peel. The Tower has been turned into an Inn named the Craster Arms, with the Craster coat of arms proudly displayed on the front of the building. The Tower is a three-storey design, with a vaulted basement. It's great to see something that was built for defence and battle has been put to such a welcome use.

Belsay Castle

The Castle or pele tower is set in the grounds of the later Belsay Hall; both are owned by the Middleton family who have been in Northumberland since the time of the Norman Conquest. The Castle was built in the late fourteenth century. It is said that Edward I stayed at Belsay as a guest of the Middletons on his way to Scotland, however the date of this is unknown and it was an earlier castle not the one we see today. This castle was probably started in the reign of Edward II when Sir Gilbert de Middleton rebelled. He held two cardinals and the Bishop of Durham elect to ransom; he was later captured and executed for the crime. The Castle and lands being forfeit were later claimed by another member of the Middleton family. Today the Castle and hall are looked after by English Heritage.

Blenkinsopp Castle

These days Blenkinsopp Castle stands amid a caravan site, just off the A69 Newcastle-Carlisle road. Blenkinsopp stands in all probability about two miles from Thirlwall Castle in southern Northumberland. The original Castle was built around the fourteeth century, using stones taken from Hadrian's Wall, which is not far away. Built by Robert Bertram, a staunch supporter of Edward III, Edward had given Robert the licence to crenellate his manor house and turn it into a castle to counter the threat from Scotland in this area. Today the castle can be viewed at all times and is cared for by English Heritage.

Brackenhill Tower)

Originally built for the notorious reiver and blackmailer Richie Graham in 1584, Brackenhill is built in the Scottish Vernacular style and it is the only one of this style on the English side of the Border. It is said that Richie employed a counterfeiter who was situated in one of the rooms within Brackenhill Tower. The Grahams lost Brackenhill after the Union of the Crowns but later reclaimed it. The tower was added to in the eighteenth and nineteenth centuries when it became a hunting lodge. It fell into disrepair until the present owners restored it to former glory and now rent it out to those who wish to stay in a great piece of border history.

Corby Castle

Standing high above the River Eden and not far from the A69 Newcastle to Carlisle road is Corby Castle, a great mansion in modern times. The original pele tower was built here in the thirteenth century by the Salkeld family, who held the manors of Great and Little Corby. In 1624 it was sold to Lord William Howard, a younger son of the Duke of Norfolk. There is some conjecture as to whether Bonnie Prince Charlie stayed at the manor in 1745, but it cannot be substantiated. The house was extended and renovated over the next two centuries by the Howard family.

Coupland Castle

The Castle stands near the junction of the River Till and the College Burn in Glendale, Northumberland, in the far west of what was the English East March. This is a late castle for the age and probably built in the late sixteenth century or the early days after the Union of the Crowns by the Wallace family who had succeeded the Coupland family as landowners of the area.

Craster Tower

Craster Tower is situated inland from the village of Craster, a tower that is held by the family of the same name as the village. The name is a pun on the name for a crow (craw) or raven which appears on the family crest. The village originally called Crawster. The Tower has been in the same family's hands since the mid twelfth century, when the family settled here from Rhineland.

Crew Castle

Very little remains of Crew Castle except for a mound and a few stones, it was however the original home of the notorious reiver Hobbie Noble. Mentioned in 1583 as the home of Will Noble, but recorded as a bastle house and not a castle. It is positioned some 120 metres south of present day Crew Farm. The remains show that the south and west facings have gun loops indicating either a later sixteenth century build or modifications later still. At some point it has had a barmkin around it. Today the Castle is used as a sheep pen.

Doddington Bastle

Today Doddington Bastle is not much more than a pile of stones in the centre of Doddington village three miles north of Wooler in Glendale, Northumberland. The Bastle was probably built in the sixteenth century to protect the farmer, his family and some of the more important cattle of the family.

Duddo Tower

Situated on the road from Ford to Berwick and only three miles from the Scottish Border, Duddo is only a ruin today. The Tower ruins sit on a crag to the south of Duddo village. The Tower does command a vast view of the surrounding area far into Scotland and the Lammermoor Hills and towards Flodden Field. The Tower originally had a barmkin protecting it. Duddo had been passed around a number of well-known border families including the Grays of Wark and the Claverings. In 1496 James IV of Scotland sacked the Tower on a raid into Northumberland in support of Perkin Warbeck's claim to the English throne.

Elsdon Tower

The Tower is situated in the middle of Elsdon village no more than 100 metres from the church. Built in the fourteenth century, originally by the de Umfraville family of southern Northumberland, it is a strong tower. The Umfravilles held this part of Redesdale and Tynedale for William the Conqueror. In 1415 it was recorded as a turret by a survey of castles done for Henry V. Listed as being attached to St Cuthbert's church, it was in all probability built to protect the priest from the numerous border raids of the time. Today the Tower is a private residence, and not open to the public. A plaque on the wall outside gives details of the Tower and some history.

Featherstone Castle

Featherstone is situated in a valley of the South Tyne, only a few miles south of Blenkinsopp Castle. Even today it is a beautiful, peaceful location and a wonderfully preserved castle. The original pele tower was built as a defence against the Scots raids, somewhere around the twelfth century. During the Civil War Sir Timothy Featherstonehaugh stood for King Charles I, who had awarded him his knighthood. Indeed it would also cost Sir Timothy his life, as he was captured and then executed after the Battle of Worcester. His estates including the Castle were forfeited to the treasury. These were then purchased by the Wallace family, owners of Blenkinsopp Castle.

Harbottle Castle

Harbottle was not built like most of the local castles by a landed and titled local family, but jointly by the Bishop of Durham and King Henry II. Being nine miles from the village of Rothbury it is indeed a remote outpost. The Castle was in the care of Odinel de Umfraville, with support from the Bishopric of Durham. The Castle was taken in a raid into Northumberland by Robert the Bruce in 1319. However 200 years later in 1515 it was in good enough order to receive Margaret Tudor, daughter of King Henry VII and sister of Henry VIII. Indeed it was at Harbottle in 1515 that Margaret gave birth to her daughter Margaret, who would become the grandmother of James VI. During Elizabethan times the Castle was held by the Dacre family, more readily connected with the English West March. Unfortunately today there is very little that remains of the Castle except one corner of a tower.

Housesteads Bastle

It can be said with some certainty that this bastle house has been built with stone from the Roman wall, it is situated within the boundaries of Housesteads Roman Fort on the Wall. The bastle was built in the early part of the sixteenth century by a member of the notorious Armstrong family, well known for their reiving exploits. Only the ground floor of the house survives today, it is in the place where the guardhouse would have been in the Roman fort. The site is looked after today by English Heritage.

Kyloe Tower

Kyloe is situated just off the A1, the Great North Road on the way from Belford to Berwick. The Tower now forms part of the farm buildings, even though it is in disrepair. The Tower was inhabited until around 1633 and held by the Gray family. In 1541 the Gray family still held it and, and in the survey of the borders it was indicated that it had a barmkin around it.

Pressen Bastle

Situated on a farm in the village of Carham, this bastle is strategically placed on the Scottish Border. The bastle is more like a fortified house with walls four and a half feet thick. In keeping with a lot of bastle houses it had a vaulted basement and the entrance to the house was by ladder to the first floor. It was recorded as a strong house in the border survey of 1541. In 1586 Christopher Dacre wrongly recorded it as being a tower and not a bastle. At that time it was held by the Gray family, today it is used as a farm workshop.

Scaleby Castle
The castle at Scaleby stands just outside the village of the same name. The Castle has developed through time with the different owners to have occupied Scaleby. It was built by the Norman Tilliol family in 1307 just after the death of Edward I when his son Edward II succeeded him. The house or manor was given a licence to crenellate by Edward II. It was at that time only a pele tower in common with a lot in the borders. The Castle passed through a number of families including the Colvilles and the Musgraves. Indeed it was Sir Edward Musgrave who held the Castle for King Charles in 1648 during the Civil War. The Castle surrendered to Parliamentarian forces after only one cannon shot. In contrast to three years earlier when it was besieged by Parliamentary forces for seven months before surrendering. Indeed the Musgrave's retained the Castle into the eighteenth century when they extended it. Today Scaleby is in private hands and not open to the public.

Tarset Castle
Four miles north of Bellingham stands the mound that once Tarset Castle stood on. The Castle was built by the Scottish knight John Comyn, often referred to as "the Black Comyn". It was built at a time of good relations between England and Scotland and as a result of the marriage of Henry III's sister Joan to Alexander II of Scotland, the two men would later define the Anglo-Scottish Border in the Treaty of York on 25 September 1237. With the murder of John Comyn's son John, known as "the Red Comyn" by Robert the Bruce, Bruce also gained Tarset Castle. The Castle in later times often suffered at the hands of Scottish raiders. In the 1541 survey of the castles in the borders it was garrisoned by Sir Ralph Fenwick.

Triermain Castle
Not much remains of Triermain Castle, save one part of a tower. Using stone from Hadrian's Wall, this Castle was built on high ground near the River Irthing when in or around 1340, Roland

Vaux was given the licence to crenellate an existing house. Triermain held sway in the Gilsland area before the castle at Askerton was built; it had ceased to be a force in the area and was in decay before the end of the sixteenth century. By the seventeenth century most of the castle was in ruins or completely demolished. The Castle and one of the many Roland Vaux who owned it are mentioned in Sir Walter Scott's novel *The Bride of Triermain*.

Wark Castle

The village of Wark is situated fifteen miles west of Berwick, where only a mound of earth remains of the castle at Wark on Tweed. During the sixteenth century the Castle was strategically important in keeping the English Border quiet. The Castle guarded one of the main fords or crossings for the River Tweed. The original castle was constructed around the twelfth century and was rebuilt on a number of occasions between the twelfth and sixteenth centuries. It is believed that the English troops under Edward II crossed the Tweed at this point on their way to Bannockburn. Wark was taken by the Scottish army under James IV on his way to Flodden, and defeat.

Caerlaverock Castle
"Maxwell's Castle of the Skylark"

Set in beautiful Dumfries and Galloway pastureland the "Fort of the Skylark", to give Caerlaverock Castle its translation from Old Scots, is a wonderful sight with the moat around its uniquely triangular structure, and probably one of the most picturesque castles in the British Isles.

Building started in 1277 for Sir Herbert Maxwell, replacing an earlier castle placed nearer the Caerlaverock burn. In 1300 when the Castle was barely twenty years old it suffered a siege at the hands of Edward I of England when he invaded Scotland with eighty-seven knights and about 3,000 men at arms. The English held Caerlaverock for the next twelve years. The Castle reverted back to the Maxwell family who changed their allegiance to Robert the Bruce, a strange choice as historically they had alliances with the Balliol family. Bruce ordered Sir Eustace Maxwell to destroy the Castle in case it fell into English hands.

In 1329 with the death of Robert and the succession of his son David, who became David II of Scotland, the Maxwells changed sides again and supported Edward Balliol, son of John. Sir Eustace Maxwell rebuilt the Castle and then garrisoned it himself.

The Maxwells began to slowly rebuild the Castle starting in around 1370; there is no record of when this work was finished. However, it must have finished prior to the latter part of the fifteenth century. When the Maxwells were created lords, Sir Herbert Maxwell being the first, they were also given the wardenry of the Scottish West March, where in later years they would rival and feud with the Johnstones.

The dawn of the sixteenth century saw the borders used as a battleground again and in particular the Battle of Flodden in 1513. The Maxwells suffered badly at Flodden losing Lord John and his three brothers. By this time the Maxwells also owned Lochmaben and Threave castles, as well as considerable lands in the area.

Robert the 5th Earl who had taken over after Flodden, held court to King James V of Scotland in 1542 prior to the Battle of Solway Moss, which ended in defeat for the King and the capture of Robert. The Castle fell to the English in 1544 with Robert again being taken prisoner. This time it only remained in English hands for a year.

In 1570 the Earl of Sussex led an English army north and Caerlaverock again fell to the English. It isn't clear at this point how long the Castle remained in English hands but it did pass back to the Maxwell family and they were strengthening the Castle defences again, in 1593.

The seventeenth century dawned with the ascension of James VI of Scotland to the English throne, making him James I of England, also known as the Union of the Crowns. This for a time brought peace of sorts to the borders and Caerlaverock.

By 1634 the Castle received more building work to turn it from a fortification into a country mansion, without removing the crenellations. When the Civil War broke out the Maxwell's sided with the King and Caerlaverock had to endure another siege, this time resisting a Covenanters' army led by Lieutenant Colonel

John Home. The Castle held out for thirteen weeks before having to surrender. After this siege the Castle was partially dismantled.

Today Caerlaverock is looked after and cared for by Historic Scotland.

The Maxwell crest, situated above the gatehouse entrance to the castle.

Cessford Castle
"The Small Tough One"

The power base of the Ker family during the fifteenth & sixteenth centuries, this castle is thought to have been built by Andrew Ker around 1450. However an older castle probably pre-dates this one on the site. Most of what we see today is how the Ker family modified it from the structure standing in 1450 until, as the Dukes of Roxburgh, they left it for Floors Castle in Kelso.

Given the Barony of Cessford in 1446 by Earl Douglas, Andrew Ker and his descendants were noted border reivers and often served as Wardens of the Scottish Middle March. Standing on high ground near to Kale Water and near to the town of Kelso. The Castle is substantially built although it is not the largest around, at some sixty feet by seventy feet. It did however have a formidable reputation: second only to its owners and, in 1523, it was thought to be the third strongest castle in Scotland. The walls in some places are fourteen feet thick. Primarily built for defence it has small windows. It also had a barmkin wall, however little of this today.

The Castle was regularly attacked by English armies in their forays into Scotland. The Earl of Surrey besieged the Castle with eleven cannons in 1523, during the "Rough Wooing" and the Castle eventually surrendered. The Castle was abandoned in 1544 after repeated English raids.

The Kers fought with most on the Border and even another branch of the family, the Kers of Ferniehirst, at some point during the centuries and would appear to have been unpopular with not only the locals but most of north Northumberland and Cumberland too, feuding with their opposite wardens from the English side.

The Castle is still in private hands but is derelict. It is unadvisable to go inside, due to the weakness of the structure.

Dryhope Tower
"The Flower of Yarrow"

The Tower is situated about half a mile north of the north-west corner of St Mary's Loch, just off what today is the Southern Upland Way, overlooking the Dryhope burn. Constructed as a four-storey tower house by the Scott family, it would have had a barmkin around it, for all that today there is no sign of the barmkin.

Built by the parents of Mary Scott, often referred to as "the Flower of Yarrow", the area where the Tower stands is the Yarrow valley. Mary was given in marriage to Walter Scott of Harden, more commonly called "Auld Wat of Harden" a noted border reiver; they married in 1576 and had seven sons. Eventually that line produced the famous poet Sir Walter Scott. The Tower then passed to Walter's family.

In 1592 the Scots aligned with Francis Stewart, Earl of Bothwell against King James VI, bringing down the wrath of the monarchy and Dryhope was burnt. However by 1613 the Tower had been rebuilt. By the latter part of the seventeenth century the

Tower was in ruins through neglect and was owned by the Scotts of Buccleuch.

Physically the Tower is of strong construction with walls between four feet and five feet thick, with both arrow slits and gun loops on the lower floor. The first two floors have vaulted ceilings. It's of an oblong construction measuring about thirty-three feet by twenty-two feet.

Today the Tower has had a steel staircase fitted as part of some remedial work. The view from the roof is spectacular. Upkeep of the Tower is looked after by the Philiphaugh Trust and is accessible via the Southern Upland Way and open all year.

Fast Castle
"Castle on an Island"

Perched on a rocky outcrop reached only by a bridge on the east coast near Coldingham, and within sight of the mighty Bass Rock, is Fast Castle It is probably one of the best naturally defended castles you could wish for and a stronghold of the Home (Hume) family. It is indeed a very romantic, if at times inhospitable place to visit.

Little remains today of the once proud Castle except a few ruined outer walls. Originally only accessible by the Castle drawbridge, today a more civilised concrete bridge allows you to cross to the ruins with the 150-feet drops on either side. Struck by lightning in 1871 it could have been the inspiration for Wolf's Crag in Sir Walter Scott's *The Bride of Lammermoor*, which was also struck by lightning. Built with a keep and a barmkin wall with gatehouse and drawbridge, there is no obvious way or sign of how the Castle may have been entered from the sea. There is no harbour or signs of a jetty visible today.

The first record of the Castle is in 1333 after the Battle of Homildon Hill near Berwick-upon-Tweed. The English captured the Castle in 1346 following an incursion into Scotland after the Battle of Neville's Cross. It remained in English hands until 1410 when Patrick Home, the Earl of Dunbar, captured it in a daring raid. A large part of the Castle was destroyed after the Battle of Flodden. The Castle then stayed in the Home family, who rebuilt large parts of it in 1521.

During the war of "the Rough Wooing" in 1547 the Castle was again taken by the English under the Earl of Somerset, who pursued the edict of Henry VIII that Mary Queen of Scots should marry the future Edward VI. Mary Queen of Scots stayed at Fast castle in 1566.

The Castle changed hands back to the Home family, but by 1570 it was back in English hands. In 1580 the Castle passed by marriage to the Logans of Restalrig, but they forfeited the Castle after their involvement in the Gowrie conspiracy of 1582, and their lands were seized by the crown. The Douglases bought the Castle from the Crown in 1602, but it saw little use and fell into a ruinous state.

Fatlips Castle
"Turnbulls on the Hill"

Standing at the top of the Minto Crag above the village of Denholm in Roxburghshire, Fatlips or Minto Castle stands proudly with wonderful views on all sides. Minto Castle was built as a pele tower, probably around 1530, to a typical Scottish tower design and was the stronghold of the Turnbull family who also had another tower at Barnhill. Over the years the Castle has been known by many names: Fatlips, Minto, Mantoncrake and Catslick. However, today it is more often known by the name Fatlips.

The style of the tower is very similar in design to a number of Scottish border pele towers among them Gilknockie, Cardonness and Smailholm.

Built on a rectangular plan measuring twenty-seven feet by thirty-two feet, it consists of three floors with an accessible parapet walk.

The name of the Castle, 'Fatlips', it is said came from the way in which the inhabitants of the Castle greeted their female guests, with less decorum than was thought fit at that time.

During the war of the Rough Wooing, the Earl of Hertford, later called Protector Somerset, burned Minto Castle in 1545. The castle was rebuilt when Henry VIII tried to get the Scottish to agree to a marriage of the infant Mary Queen of Scots to his son Prince Edward, later Edward VI.

The Yett or Iron gate at Fatlips

Ferniehirst Castle
"Scotland's Alamo"

   Built in 1470 by the Ker (or Kerr) family, the original castle was the tower house that now forms the basis of the later L-shaped castle plan we see today. Situated about two miles south of Jedburgh and near the banks of the Jed Water, it is today home to Sir Ralf Kerr and his family. The Castle is fronted on its approach by two bastle houses, one of which is complete and houses the visitor centre, the other is in ruins with only two walls standing. These were built around 1540, most likely by the English, who occupied the Castle at this time and gave a strong defensive approach position to the Castle.

   As the stature of the Ker family increased in the borders so the house was added to, so the present structure is the result of many additions and modifications. The Castle was originally within the confines of the Jed Forrest and was given to the Ker family as vassals of the 4th Earl of Angus, George Douglas. The Jed Forrest lands included Ferniehirst; here the Kers would protect the Scottish Border for Angus. Sir Thomas Ker had his home at Smailholm (later Pringle territory); on receiving the lands at Ferniehirst he built the tower.

Sir Thomas was succeeded by his son Andrew 'Dand' Ker in 1499, who consolidated the Kers land and reputation in the borders. Set in a backdrop of wars against the English Dand Ker was well equipped for this as a seasoned border fighter. Sir Andrew was considered loyal to the Scottish crown and in 1502 gained the barony of Oxnam; he was also appointed the Warden of the Scottish Middle March. Sir Andrew was not averse to a spot of reiving, together with other notable families of the borders.

One of two Bastle houses situated at the entrance to the castle, this one is now the visitor centre.

In 1523 Ferniehirst was captured by Thomas Howard, Earl of Surrey and Lord Dacre, for the English, during one of the many raids to get the Scots to submit to the will of Henry VIII. At the same time vast areas of Teviotdale and Jedburgh Abbey were destroyed. At this time Sir Andrew Ker lived for the majority of the time in Edinburgh. The English came north again in 1544.

The battle that ensued the next year at Ancrum Moor just north of Jedburgh ended in the English being routed and both their commanders on the day, Sir Brian Layton and Sir Ralph Eure, were killed. However Ferniehirst stayed in English hands.

Ferniehirst remained in English hands until July 1548 when it was relieved by a force of French who were assisting the Scots. At the time the Castle was garrisoned by around eighty soldiers. The French undermined the Castle and used gunpowder to gain access; the English then decided it would be better to surrender to the French than the advancing Scottish army. The French duly accepted the surrender, but promptly sold the captured English to the Scots. They in turn took revenge and tortured and executed the prisoners, mounting the heads on spears. There is a famous poem by Walter Laidlaw which details the French relief of Ferniehirst.

The Castle was returned to the Kers after the relief and into the hands of John Ker. John Ker was knighted later that year by Regent Arran, he was then duly appointed as Warden of the Middle March, and he died at Ferniehirst in 1562.

In 1568 Sir Thomas Ker rode at the side of Mary, Queen of Scots in the battle of Langside near Glasgow. In fact in 1566 Mary had stayed in a Ker house in Jedburgh whilst visiting Lord Bothwell in Hermitage Castle. In 1569 after the failed rising of the northern Earls in England, Ferniehirst acted as a refuge for the Earl of Westmorland.

After the Union of the Crowns the Castle became a home and what was a bastle house and is now the visitor centre was converted into a chapel.

During World War II Ferniehirst was home to the Royal Artillery; unfortunately they removed a lot of the original doors and used them for firewood. Later in the 1960s and 1970s it became a youth hostel, it was returned to a home in the 1980s by the 12th Lord Lothian.

Today Ferniehirst is a private residence. However, during the riding month of July it opens its doors and guided tours are available.

Gilnockie Tower
"Home of Black Jock"

Gilknockie or Hollows Tower (sometimes known as Holehouse) sits high above the River Esk, near Canonbie, in what was known as the Debateable Lands. Often referred to as the spiritual home of the Armstrong family, Gilnockie was once the home of the noted reiver Johnnie Armstrong, younger brother of Thomas Armstrong of Mangerton. Often known as "Black Jock", he was a noted reiver and freebooter.

Built around 1520 by Johnnie Armstrong, it is said to get its original name of Hollows Tower from the large hollow in the ground beside it. This it is said is where they dug out the stone from which to build the Tower house. Sir Christopher Dacre raided and burnt the Tower in the 1530s, and the Tower was rebuilt in the 1540s. Johnnie was granted the lands by Lord Maxwell in return for "Man Rent" or to be a soldier when Maxwell required him. Johnnie was hung along with about thirty of his followers at Caerlenrigg by the young James V of Scotland, in 1530, in a purge of reivers.

By 1547 it is thought that Gilknockie was in the hands of Sandy Armstrong, who was known to side with the English in the ongoing cross-border raids. It was still in Sandy's hands when the Border was divided in 1552 by the French Ambassador, due to whose definition it put Gilknockie firmly on Scottish soil.

In 1579 the Tower was owned by another Johnnie Armstrong. Johnnie held it until around 1623 when it passed to an Archie Armstrong. At some point modifications must have been made to accommodate the basement gun-loop for the defence of the Tower.

In 1978 the Tower was in a ruinous state with no roof. It was then bought by Major T C R Armstrong-Wilson. Major Armstrong-Wilson set about restoring the Tower to its former glory days, replacing the doors with oak ones and re-roofing. Today it houses the Armstrong Clan Museum.

Greenknowe Tower
"Setons Retreat"

Situated in the village of Gordon, five miles north-east of Earlston in Berwickshire this restored four-storey tower house sits on a low mound. Built in 1581 by James Seton for himself and his wife Janet Edmonstone, their initials are engraved above the door together with their respective coats of arms.

Alexander Seton had acquired the land around in the early fifteenth century, in all likelihood from the Gordons who had settled here earlier from their powerbase in north-east Scotland, they were granted the land by Malcolm II in 1018. The Seton's married into the Gordon family at a later date.

In the seventeenth century the Tower was sold to Robert Pringle of Stichel in 1637, in fact Richard's son, the noted Covenanter William Pringle (he is also recorded as Walter) who fought at the Battle of Dunbar against Cromwell, resided in the Tower for a while in the 1660s. By the nineteenth century the Tower had been abandoned as a residence and fell into disrepair, it was uninhabitable by 1830 and a century later it passed into state hands.

The L-shaped tower is constructed of rubble-type stone in the traditional building style of the late sixteenth century. There is earthwork evidence that there originally had been a barmkin wall surrounding the Tower, of which there are no remains today. The main part of the Tower is thirty-four feet by twenty-two feet, the walls being four feet thick. The wing of the Tower measures eleven feet by fifteen feet, giving very comfortable living accommodation. It has bartizan turrets in the north-west and south-east corners.

An interesting point of the tower is the main stairs, which are counter clockwise or left handed. A feature which is often attributed to houses and castles associated with the Kerr family, which is odd as there is no connection between Greenknowe and the Kerr family.

Today Greenknowe is in the keeping of Historic Scotland and open and free for all to see.

Hermitage Castle
"The Strength of Liddesdale"

Standing isolated and alone in the valley of Liddesdale just across the Scottish border are the towering ruins of Hermitage Castle, so often referred to as "the Strength of Liddesdale" or more disparagingly "Sod Off in Stone". It is a bleak ruin standing in a bleak location and majestic in its own grimness. To any that had to garrison it or those who chose to attack, it wasn't a pleasant site. Even worse for those who were taken prisoner and held here, in particular in the depths of winter.

During the reiving times this was the base for the Keeper of Liddesdale, definitely an impossible job in that they had to keep law and order in a lawless society.

The Castle was originally built by Nicholas de Soulis, a rather unsavoury fellow who by all accounts was as grim as his castle and lasting monument. He built the Castle around 1240, as a motte and bailey construction like so many castles of that century. The Castle stayed in the de Soulis family until around

1320, when William de Soulis was suspected of witchcraft and had his lands and castle forfeited to the Scottish crown. It appeared that William de Soulis was as equally unsavoury as his predecessor and upset most of the locals. Legend has it that they captured him and took him to the nearby Nine Stane Rig and wrapped him in lead and boiled him in a large cauldron, he didn't appear to cause any more problems after that. The story is a good one however, in reality he was taken prisoner by King Robert I of Scotland and died in Dumbarton Castle prison.

Some time after this the Castle passed into English hands, although it isn't clear exactly when. But in 1338 the Castle was held by Sir Ralph de Neville. He was besieged, inside the Castle, that year by Sir William Douglas, of the Black Douglas family, of the Scottish West March. After his death the Castle passed to another William Douglas of the same family. Briefly after this the Dacres of Narworth in Westmorland held the Castle but it reverted back to the Douglases until after the Battle of Arkinholme in 1455 and the demise of the Black Douglases. The Castle then reverted to King James II of Scotland who gave it to another Douglas family, this time the Earls of Angus better known as the Red Douglases.

This branch of the Douglas family earned the suspicion of James IV with the relationship of Angus to Henry VII of England. One of the outcomes of this suspicion was that he was ordered to surrender Hermitage to the Crown. This he did. The Castle and its surrounding lands were then given, by charter, to Patrick Hepburn, 1st Earl Bothwell. Bothwell then became Keeper of Liddesdale.

The Hepburns kept the Castle and lands until it came into the hands of James Hepburn, 4th Earl of Bothwell who was the lover of Mary, Queen of Scots. She rode sixty miles to visit him after he had an unfortunate entanglement with "Wee Jock of the Park"; she unfortunately took ill after this ride and stayed for some time in a Kerr house in Jedburgh, known today as Queen Mary's house. Bothwell fled to Norway after Mary was forced to abdicate; he forfeited all his lands and titles.

Francis Bothwell the nephew of James Bothwell was the next keeper of the castle. Unfortunately for him he was implicated in the North Berwick witch trials for which he was arrested and forfeited the lands, and they were never to be held by the family again. The Castle then reverted to the Scottish crown and James VI.

The Castle was awarded to Walter Scott of Buccleuch (the bold Buccleuch of Kinmont Willie fame) in 1594, who at the time was the Warden of the Scottish Marches and Keeper of Liddesdale. The Castle would stay in the Scott family until 1930 when it would be handed over to the Crown for preservation. Today the Castle is looked after by Historic Scotland and is open in the summer months.

Home (Hume) Castle

Home Castle stands on a mound or motte situated between the village of Greenlaw and the town of Kelso and two miles north of the village of Stichill. It was the main power base in the East March of the Home (Hume) family who controlled the Eastern March. The earliest parts of the Castle date from the early thirteenth century when in 1215 the 6th Earl of Dunbar and March granted the lands to his daughter, Ada, upon her marriage to William Greenlaw, who then became William of Home. The mound the Castle sits on is indeed impressive, commanding views all round and is in a very defensible position.

The present Castle would have been started around the time of Ada and would have been expanded and improved upon over the coming centuries, indeed in 1313 when Robert the Bruce instigated his scorched earth policy against the English, prior to the Battle of Bannockburn, Home Castle was left standing when others in the borders where fired or demolished.

In 1460 during the siege of Roxburgh Castle, which was held at the time by the English, James II and his queen Mary of Gueldres stayed in Home Castle. The outcome didn't go well for

James as he died of wounds sustained when a cannon blew up as he lit the fuse.

During the early 1540s the Homes used the French to improve the defences at Home Castle, adding gun loops and strengthening the ramparts. In 1547 the Duke of Somerset took the Castle for the English, but it was in English hands for less than a year when the 4th Lord Home retook the Castle putting the entire garrison to the sword.

The Castle was again taken by the English in 1569 when the Earl of Sussex invaded Scotland on behalf of Queen Elizabeth, after the rising of the northern earls and Lord Home's support for Mary, Queen of Scots. The Castle surrendered within twelve hours, this time the English held the Castle for three years. After this the Homes were given a grant by Regent Morton to keep the Castle for James VI.

The downfall of the Castle came during the War of the Three Kingdoms (English Civil War) when it was held for the Crown by Sir John Cockburn and attacked and destroyed by a Cromwellian force under the command of Colonel Fenwick.

During the Napoleonic wars there was a beacon station held at the Castle, one night on 31 January 1804 the sergeant in charge saw what they thought of as beacons in the distance and lit the Home beacon. This triggered what was known as "the Great Alarm" with over 3,000 men mustered. It turned out to be a false alarm and the French invasion never came.

Today the Castle is still the spiritual home of the Home (Hume) family and in 1929 the Castle and the surrounding land was purchased for the crown. However, in 2005 the Castle was purchased by the Home family trust bringing the Castle back in to Home hands after 100 years.

Kirkhope Tower

Standing alone on a hillside and situated beautifully in the Ettrick Valley, just north of Ettrick village is Kirkhope Tower. The original tower was built in the early part of the sixteenth century for the Scott family. In 1547 it was burnt in a raid by the Armstrongs, when all the cattle and furniture were taken. In all probability the Armstrongs were encouraged by the English as part of the Rough Wooing that Henry VIII was conducting at the time. It was rebuilt by Auld Wat of Harden in the late sixteenth century, probably around 1578.

The Tower is a four-storey construction with two turrets on the roof and a vaulted ground floor, with an oblong layout measuring approximately twenty-three feet by twenty-eight feet. The ground floor would have been where the cattle or horses would have been kept during a raid and only a small door, one cow wide, is the access to this floor. The first floor would have been accessed by a wooden ladder that would have been pulled up during raiding times. This led directly into the great hall of the Tower, where most of the daily business would be conducted, at night servants would often sleep here. The second and third floors of the Tower were for the laird and his family and included sleeping quarters.

It may have been that Kirkhope was one of the towers constructed just after 1535, by order of an act of the Scottish Parliament ordering large landowners to build towers with barmkin, the barmkin being sixty feet in area. The remains of a barmkin still exist, in parts, around the Tower. A map by William Roy in 1750 showed the barmkin was still in existence.

Occupation of the Tower was continuous until the late seventeenth century, when it fell into disrepair. It was then bought and restored in the 1990s, is now in private hands and not open to the general public.

Langholm Castle
"Armstrong's Last Ride"

Little remains of Langholm Castle today, only a large part of the south wall of the main tower. In its heyday it had a barmkin and outer buildings. Built on a flat piece of land near the centre of Langholm town centre and the confluence of the Rivers Esk and Ewes, it is strange that it is built on flat land and not high up as would have been more normal. It can only be thought that the builder thought that they were safe. Indeed the builder was Christopher Armstrong, brother of Johnny "Black Jock" Armstrong so, with the strength of the surrounding Armstrong family in the Debateable Lands, he would have felt very safe when he built the Castle in 1526.

The position of the Castle is in the centre of Langholm racecourse and a stone's throw from the Armstrong Museum. The tower originally measured forty-two feet by thirty feet, with walls six feet thick and would have had three floors.

It is thought that Johnnie Armstrong rode out from Langholm Castle in 1530 to meet the young King James V and this ultimately ended in Johnnie and his followers' execution at Caerlenrigg on the road to Hawick, What isn't known is whether his brother accompanied him on this fateful journey. If he did it is likely the Castle passed into royal hands. It did later pass into the ownership of the Scott family. Captured in 1544 by the English on one of the many raids into Scotland, it was retaken into Scottish hands in 1547. In fact, the Castle changed hands regularly throughout the 1500s. In 1596 it was the start of more intrigue since it was where the rescue of Kinmont Willie was discussed and planned.

The Castle was destroyed in 1603 after the Union of the Crowns either by or on the orders of James VI. Today the Castle is owned by the Duke of Buccleuch and cared for by the Armstrong trust.

Lochmaben Castle
"Started by Bruce, finished by Edward"

The Bruce (de Brus) family built the original castle south of the current structure. What remains of this castle lies under the second green of the golf course; the construction was probably of wood and built around 1160. The second later castle built on the shores of Castle Loch south of the town of Lochmaben. This thirteenth-century castle was a more substantial structure.

In 1298 the Castle was built by Edward I of England. This gave Edward a base in the south-west of Scotland in his quest to conquer Scotland. It is clear by the remains of the ruins we see today that the castle Edward built was a complex and sturdy one, protected on one side by the loch.

Bruce retook the Castle in 1306, but didn't hold it for long before it was retaken by the English. After the Battle of Bannockburn in 1314, the Castle was handed back to the Scots along with other English-held castles in the south of Scotland.

The English returned after the Battle of Halidon Hill near Berwick in 1333 and retook the Castle, holding it for the next sixty years. In 1384 after a siege of nine days Sir Archibald Douglas (Archibald the Grim) succeeded in taking the Castle with help from the Earls of March and Douglas. The Castle became the possession of the Earls of March; however the Earls fell out of favour with the Scottish Royal Family. The relationship was repaired by the 10th Earl and his lands and titles were reinstated, except for the Lordship of Annandale and the Castle at Lochmaben in 1409.

With the show of strength by James II to wrest power from the McDonalds the Lords of the Isles and the Black Douglases in south-west Scotland, the Castle was besieged and taken after the defeat of the Douglases at the Battle of Arkinholme in June 1455. After the Battle of Lochmaben Fair, fought on 22 July 1484, between supporters of James III and the rebels, James Douglas the 9th Earl Douglas and Alexander Stewart, Duke of Albany, the Castle was held for James, with the defeat of the rebels, who had been supported by Edward IV of England.

James IV spent his honeymoon at Lochmaben Castle and added the great hall to it in 1503. In 1542, James V resided at the Castle and gathered his forces before the March into England and defeat at the Battle of Solway Moss. In 1565 Mary, Queen of Scots stayed at the Castle and attended a banquet with her first husband Lord Darnley. James VI besieged the Castle in 1588, whilst it was held by the Maxwell family, after the Maxwells support for the Catholic religion and the attempt to overthrow the Protestant monarchy of Scotland. Lord David Maxwell held out at Lochmaben until James brought forth artillery, either purchased or borrowed from England's Queen Elizabeth. The Castle surrendered after five days, Maxwell was hung in front of the Castle. Queen Mary's nephew the Earl of Bothwell briefly took the Castle in 1592, but he didn't hold it for long.

Warden courts were held often at the Castle and it was used by the wardens of the West March during their tenure in office. So it was in 1600 when Sir John Carmichael was headed to Lochmaben for such a court when he was murdered by Armstrongs at Mosspaul. They were all later caught and hung.

With the Union of the Crowns in 1603 the Castle was no longer required and after a few years it fell into disrepair. Unfortunately it is but a ruin and shadow of its former glory.

Lochwood Tower

Lochwood is the family seat of the Johnstone clan, and was prominent during the reiving period, indeed the current ruins probably date from the late fifteenth or early sixteenth century. It is situated a few miles to the south-west of Moffatt in Dumfriesshire in what was the Scottish West March.

There has probably been a castle on this ground since the twelfth century when John was granted the surrounding lands by Robert de Brus, who was Lord of Annandale. At this time, in all likelihood, it would be a wooden motte and bailey type of structure. Slowly the wood was replaced by stone to strengthen the defences. As the records of the early years of the Castle, or more likely a well-fortified tower house, were destroyed by fire in 1585, no actual descriptions prior to this date exist. The area would become known as "Johns Toun" and later Johnston.

During the Scottish War of Independence Gilbert de Johnstone the son of Jon swore fealty to Edward I in 1296, for this loyalty he was awarded lands in the borders. This gave them a more prominent role in border affairs. By 1398, Sir John Johnstone was made Warden of the West March, a position of some authority in the Border. It is thought that the stone castle had been built around 1380 to replace the wooden structure. The Johnstones continued to use Lochwood as the primary residence and grow in stature within the Scottish West March.

During 1455 the Johnstones assisted James II with the suppression of the Black Douglases first at the Battle of Arkinholme near Langholme and then in the siege of Threave Castle.

The Tower was captured by English in 1544, who reported Lochwood as a good strong tower with a substantial barmkin. The English arrived by night whilst Sir James Johnstone was a prisoner in England, so the Tower was only lightly guarded. The English were led by Sir Thomas Carleton, who with about twelve men scaled the barmkin wall. They got close to the Tower and took prisoner some of the women housed in the outer area, they kept them until daybreak. They waited for the tower door on the inside to be opened and then rushed it so that it couldn't be closed with reinforcements joining them from the outside of the wall to assist in taking the Tower. The English used it as their base in 1547 and for a further three years, it remained in Sir Thomas Carleton's possession.

The Tower was listed in the survey done for the English by Lord Wharton, known as the "Platte of Castlemilk" which listed and included sketches of all the main strongholds in the Scottish borders.

Burnt by the Maxwells in 1585 during the long-running feud of the two prominent Scottish families culminating in the Battle of Dryfe Sands near Lockerbie in December 1593. It's claimed that it was with the keys of Lochwood that Lady Johnstone struck the fatal blow to Lord Maxwell either during or just after the Battle.

With the Union of the Crowns in 1603 the fortification became less important and other residences nearer Edinburgh were used, the tower being recorded as being used until the beginning of the eighteenth century, when it fell into disrepair.

The Tower today lies in ruins and is very overgrown. It was excavated in 1969 by Alasdair M T Maxwell-Irving, and again in 1980 by the Earl of Annandale, who had a considerable amount of rubble cleared. It is still in the hands of the Hope-Johnstone family.

Morton Castle

Standing on a large mound high above an elbow in Morton Loch, it's as if the Loch has wrapped its watery arms around the ground beneath the Castle and lovingly squeezed until the mound has risen and the Castle perched on its summit. Set in a peaceful glen, it's not difficult to sit and imagine the clatter of horses' hooves echoing around while a raid is on

The original castle on this site probably dates to around 1260. Later, during the reign of Robert the Bruce, Thomas Randolph, later to become first Earl of Moray, developed the site and castle. Unfortunately under the Treaty of Berwick, signed to obtain the release of David II in 1357, a number of castles had to be destroyed in Nithsdale, and Morton was chosen to be one of them. How well or to what extent this was done and how much remained is unknown.

The Castle and the lands of Morton passed into the hands of the Earls of March in 1440. They rebuilt the Castle in the fifteenth century, and much of what we see today is due to them. In the mid fifteenth century the Castle was given, by James II, to James Douglas, later Earl of Morton.

During the sixteenth century, Morton had a chequered history. The start of the century saw the Castle still held by the Douglases. However, the fourth Earl was beheaded for his part in the murder of Lord Darnley, husband of Mary, Queen of Scots. The Castle was then passed to the Maxwell family when they were wardens of the West March. In 1588 the Castle was under the ownership of James Maxwell, a noted Catholic sympathiser when James VI led a raid on Morton and against the Catholic Maxwells. The Castle was burned and its ownership returned to the Earls of Morton.

During the sixteenth century, Morton was first sold back to the Douglas family in the guise of William Douglas of Coshogle, who then sold it to William Douglas of Drumlanrig, who later became the Marquis of Queensbury. At this time the Castle was still occupied to some degree. The Castle was eventually abandoned in the eighteenth century and allowed to fall into disrepair.

The Castle bears a striking resemblance to Caerlaverock on which it could possibly have been styled. There is no sign of a barmkin if there has been one at any time. The Loch is artificial in that it was done in the late eighteenth century by placing a dam and flooding the surrounding marshland that actually was used as a defensive mechanism for the Castle.

The Castle today is owned by the Duke of Buccleuch and cared for by Historic Scotland.

Neidpath Castle

Standing high above the River Tweed just outside the town of Peebles, Neidpath Castle is the first and most northerly in a chain of castles that are spread down the length of Tweeddale. Built on the site of an earlier castle dating from around the late twelfth century, the present Castle is an imposing tower house of sixteenth century design, although the oldest parts of the current structure date from the fourteenth century.

Sir Gilbert Fraser built a castle here in around 1190 when he held the office of Sheriff of Tweeddale. He was followed by his son Sir Simon Fraser and then his grandson, also Sir Simon Fraser, who was executed alongside William Wallace in 1307. At this point Neidpath passed into the Hey family by marriage and would stay in the family for the next two centuries.

The Castle was visited by Mary, Queen of Scots in 1563 and then by her son James VI in 1587 before the Union of the Crowns.

John Graham Marquis of Montrose is thought to have taken refuge in Niedpath after the defeat of his forces at the Battle of Philiphaugh near Selkirk in 1645, during the Civil War. Cromwell invaded Scotland in 1650 and sent a force under General Lambert to take Neidpath. It is here that there is some conflict, as some say the Castle surrendered without a shot being taken; others say that the Castle held out longer than any other castle in the Scottish borders. The Hey family were noted Royalists and would have sided with Charles I.

When Charles II ascended to the throne, he bestowed the title of Earl of Tweeddale on the 8th Lord Hey; however after renovating parts of Niedpath he fell upon hard times and was forced to sell the Castle in 1686 to William Douglas, the first Duke of Queensbury. The Duke's second son William married Lady Jean Hey, who was brought up in her formative years at Neidpath. The marriage allowed her to return to her childhood home, which had been given to her husband by her father-in-law.

It is thought that a ghost walks the Castle. It is called "the maid of Neidpath" and thought to be Jean Douglas, the youngest daughter of William Douglas and Lady Jean. After not being permitted to marry the son of the Lord of Tushielaw, she pined for him and became a shadow of herself so that, when he returned from exile, he didn't recognise her. It is thought that when Sir

Walter Scott visited the historian Adam Ferguson at Niedpath in 1803 he was told the tale and wrote about it.

Eventually the Castle passed into the hands of the Earls of Wemyss, who still own the Castle today. It is used as both a film location and a wedding venue. Tours are arranged privately.

Queen Mary's House

Situated in the centre of Jedburgh and now housing a museum to Mary, Queen of Scots' visit to Jedburgh in 1566, the house belongs to the Kers of Ferniehirst; their castle is situated just south of Jedburgh off the A68. Built on four floors in the traditional Scottish tower-house style, it shows the left-handed stairs the Kers were famous for.

Mary visited Jedburgh which often hosted royal courts to visit her lover James Hepburn, Earl of Bothwell who at the time was serving as the keeper of Liddesdale at Hermitage Castle. He also held the position of Lord Warden of the Marches. Essentially he held rule over all other Scottish march wardens.

Bothwell had an unfortunate incident with the notorious Elliot 'Wee Jock of the Park' when he was badly wounded by Jock's dagger. Mary, who was staying at the House at the time, rode the thirty miles to and from Hermitage to visit the injured Bothwell. On the ride Mary fell from her horse in poor weather. She fell ill on her return and spent some months near death, her recuperation happened in Jedburgh. The House may well have been where she recuperated, however it is also said that a bastle house was placed at her disposal. If this is true then there are two bastle houses at the entrance to Ferniehirst Castle and this is more likely where she stayed, however the legend persists.

Today the magnificently restored tower house, houses memorabilia from Mary and tells the story of the ill-fated Queen of Scots until her death, under the executioner's axe at Fotheringay Castle.

Repentance Tower

On Trailtrow Hill, within sight of Hoddam Castle and a few miles from Ecclefechan stands the Repentance Tower, surrounded by a barmkin wall which also encloses a small graveyard. Built for Sir John Maxwell, the 4th Lord Terres of Teregels as a watchtower for the castle in around 1560.

Built on three floors with no noticeable latrines and no fireplaces, meaning that it is a folly and he had never intended for anyone to live there, its name Repentance signifies he sought some sort of forgiveness, but for what is not exactly known.

It is thought that it was for a deed where, for a sum of money, in 1548 Maxwell lined up for the English with the Douglases. The night before the Battle of Druisdeer Maxwell changed sides and opposed the English. This led to the death at Carlisle Castle of twelve of his kinsmen, including his twelve-year-old nephew.

Another theory reports that it is in penitence for cutting the throats of English prisoners held in Hoddom Castle.

The third theory is that Maxwell built Hoddom Castle out of stone from the Trailtrow chapel which was originally built near the Tower. Whichever theory you believe it makes for interesting reading.

There is a stairway leading from the basement to the parapet, which is very basic, compared with other towers of the time. There is a stance for a beacon at the top of the parapet to light and warn of raiders which leads to the watchtower theory.

In later times the Tower passed to the Murray family, who emigrated. John Murray however returned with a young slave. The slave's grave is at the graveyard at Repentance.

Hoddom Castle, where the lookout at Repentance was controlled from. Repentance can be seen from the grounds of Hoddom Castle.

Roxburgh Castle

Situated a mile west from the town of Kelso and between the rivers Teviot and Tweed lies the royal castle of Roxburgh. It is within sight of the far more grandiose Floors Castle, home of the Duke of Roxburgh. Roxburgh Castle gives no clue to its royal and important past as the residence of five Scottish kings. There has been a castle here centuries before, as far back as the Saxons, taking advantage of its strong defensive position. This Castle was built for David I, who built significantly in the borders.

The Castle was lost to the English in 1174 by William the Lion as a guarantee, after his capture in the Battle of Alnwick in Northumberland. His ransom had been set at £100,000, a phenomenal sum at that time. It was back in Scottish hands in 1189 when Richard I sold the Castle and Berwick to raise money to undertake the Third Crusade. At this point Roxburgh had a town of its own with a royal mint, the town was situated between the Castle and the River Tweed.

A hundred years later and the Castle was back in English hands when John Balliol gave the Castle in homage to Edward I. It remained in English hands for over a hundred years, until Sir James the 'Black Douglas' took the Castle with only sixty men by creeping in black cloaks like cattle, then scaling the walls of the Castle.

In 1460 James II lost his life while besieging Roxburgh Castle when, after waiting for his young queen to arrive, he wanted to show his new armaments off and insisted on lighting the powder on the great cannon called "The Lion". He was standing too close and when the cannon exploded it killed him. James's queen, Mary of Guilders, continued with the siege and when the Castle had been captured she had parts of the Castle destroyed. The death of James II at Roxburgh set in the demise of both the Castle and the town.

The Castle was garrisoned by the English in 1545 during the period known as the Rough Wooing. In 1550 the Scots retook the Castle and destroyed it, not wanting the English to use it in anger again.

Today the Castle stands within the vast grounds of Floors Castle.

Smailholm Tower

Built in the traditional Scottish tower-house style of the late fifteenth and early sixteenth centuries, Smailholm, near Kelso, is associated with two notable Scottish reiving families. One was the Pringles who built it and then later the Scotts of Harden, ancestors of the writer Sir Walter Scott.

Thought to have been built around 1530 just before the onset of the Rough Wooing. Smailholm has 3 floors with a stone stair onto the roof with a placement for a fire to be lit to warn the surrounding area of an imminent reiving raid.

The Tower stands on Smailholm Craig (Scots for rock) not far from Sandyknowe Farm. This prominent position gives great views to the Cheviots in the south and the Eildon Hills in the north. It is further protected by a barmkin wall some six feet thick surrounding it, which would be the first line of defence should a raid happen. The cattle would be brought inside this wall and the more important or expensive cattle and horses would be brought into the ground floor of the Tower.

The Tower had a small thick wooden door, protected by a steel lattice door known as a *yett*. The top floors would be the residence and sleeping quarters of the laird and his family, with servants or retainers sleeping on the lower floors.

The Pringles acquired Smailholm in the mid fifteenth century, when George Pringle was connected to the Black Douglases and acted as squire for them. This had brought the Pringles wealth and power in the area. Like all families in the borders, the Pringles supplied fighting men for King James IV at the Battle of Flodden in 1513, so it was that David Pringle lost his eldest son also called David and three brothers in the Battle.

The Tower suffered repeatedly from raiders from Northumberland, in particular from Tynedale and Redesdale. It also suffered during the many excursions of the English army during the 1540s.

After becoming allies to the English and, often referred to as assured Scot's (this meant they were paid by the English Crown), for service to the English Crown to try and protect his family, John Pringle further strengthened the Tower in 1550 by inserting a gun hole to fire out over the entrance. John Pringle was in fact the last laird of Smailholm, dying in 1564.

In the 1570s Andrew Pringle left Smailholm to live in Galashiels and let out the Tower to another member of the family. Andrew's son, James, died in 1599 bankrupt and as a result of the death duties the Tower was sold to the Scotts of Harden.

In 1640 the tower was briefly occupied by the Covenanters, led by Sir Andrew Ker, during the war with Charles I. By 1720 the Tower was abandoned for some two centuries until its restoration. Today the Tower is cared for by Historic Scotland.

Threave Castle
"The Grim's Seat"

Although there are castles further west than Threave, it is probably the one furthermost west that is associated with reiving and a reiving family, that being the Black Douglases. Threave is in an idyllic position both from a defensive position and photographically, being situated on a small island in the middle of the River Dee.

There was a fortress here prior to the current Castle. It was built in around 1100 by Fergus the Celtic Earl of Galloway, That Castle was destroyed in 1308 by Robert the Bruce. In all likelihood it was probably of wooden construction and no trace of it remains.

The Castle, as it is called, although it is more like an early tower house, being constructed after the Wars of Independence, was built by Sir Archibald Douglas 'the Grim', the Third Earl of Douglas and later Lord of Galloway in around 1370. The nickname 'The Grim' came from his attitude of being merciless in battle to his enemies and not to having a miserable disposition.

The name 'Threave' is derived from old Welsh *Tref* meaning 'homestead'.

To access Threave Island has to be either by boat as tourists do today or by a small ford on the south side of the Island. It is entirely possible that the Island was inhabited for centuries prior to Sir Archibald's building his castle here in 1370. He also held Bothwell Castle from 1362 and rebuilt that castle at the same time.

Threave was the Douglases power base in Galloway for the next seventy years. It was strengthened in around 1447 to hold guns and withstand cannon, with the outer wall or barmkin being lowered, to give a clear firing line from the Castle. It also gave more of a target to the enemies outside with cannon. This proved to be the case in 1455 when, after the defeat of the Douglases at the Battle of Arkinholme near Langholm, James II besieged the Castle with cannon, supervising the siege himself. Threave held out for several months before surrendering. The ordinance for this siege came all the way from Linlithgow. The Castle was then forfeited to the Scottish crown.

The ill-fated King James IV visited the Castle in 1501, who would lose his life at the Battle of Flodden in 1513. When the keeper of the Castle, Sir James Dunbar of Blackcrag was also killed at Flodden, the castle was then looked after by the Maxwells who were wardens of the West March at that time on behalf of the King, under the stewardship of Kirkcudbright.

In 1544 the Castle briefly fell into English hands during the Rough Wooing. It was again besieged by Covenanters in 1640 when it was held by the Royalists, a siege lasting thirteen weeks. Finally it was used as a prison in the early 1800s to house captives from the Napoleonic wars.

Today, Threave is a peaceful place in the careful custody of Historic Scotland.

Torthorwald Castle
"Constant Change"

The remains of the tower at Torthorwald stand just outside Lochmaben on the road to Dumfries. Built on a small hill where an earlier motte and bailey had stood, the present castle dates from the thirteenth century and thought to be built by David de Torthorwald who was witness to a Bruce charter in 1250.

Torthorwald means "the Hill of Torold" and the family that controlled this area were the de Torthorwald family, having taken their name from the surrounding area. The first castle would have been a wooden motte and bailey type constructed around the twelfth century.

In the thirteenth century when the Bruce family were lords of Annandale the de Torthowalds witnessed a charter in 1250 and were given lands. These were subsequently revoked and given to Sir John de Soulis after the de Torthowald family supported Edward I in the first war of Scottish independence. Sir John unfortunately didn't have the lands and Castle long before he was killed in Ireland.

In 1321 Bruce granted the barony and lands of Torthowald to Sir Humphrey Kirkpatrick, the eldest son and heir of Sir Roger Kirkpatrick, who had married Isobel de Torthowald, the daughter of Sir David de Torthowald and his only heir. The lands were then confirmed along with others further north in 1326. It is possible that the stone tower house dates from around this time. Humphrey left the Castle in 1332 and fled to England when Edward Balliol invaded Scotland for his right to the Scottish throne. When Humphrey died in 1357, whilst in England as a hostage for David II, he was succeeded by his younger brother, Roger.

Roger was unfortunately murdered in Caerlaverock Castle whilst acting as captain there, he left no male heir. The estate was divided between his daughters. Elizabeth, the eldest of the three daughters inherited the Castle, she later married William Carlyle of Carlisle. William exchanged lands with Thomas Graham of Auchencass who had married Elizabeth's sister, Janet. This exchange was Elizabeth's lands for half of the lands of Roucan which had been left to Janet and on marriage passed to Thomas Graham. William died in 1463 and was succeeded by his son John who served the Scottish crown in a number of roles, eventually being created Lord Carlyle of Torthowald in 1473. John died around 1500 when the estate then passed to his grandson William.

William did not enjoy the title for long, dying in 1525, leaving his widow Janet. The title passed to his younger brother, Michael, who became the 4th Lord Carlyle. In 1547 Sir Michael pledged over 200 men to the English cause and surrendered the Castle to the English. His finances and, with them, the Castle were deteriorating and by 1565 there were only ten horsemen left at the Castle. The lands and Castle were sold in around 1573, with his son remaining as a tenant.

After Sir Michael's death in 1575, the Castle and lands were contested between his son Michael and his second son's daughter Elizabeth. This dispute required the intervention of the Regent Morton, who despite Michael's protests and the fact that he had legally purchased the lands two years earlier gave the lands to his half-brother George Douglas of Parkhead. Michael, refusing to move out, was "put to the horn".

Morton's fall from grace in 1580 meant that George Douglas had lost his biggest supporter. The Castle and lands were awarded to the Douglases in 1583 but then revoked by James VI. They were then given to John Johnstone who was Warden of the West March at the time.

Sir John imprisoned the noted reiver and blackmailer Richie Graham of Brackenhill in Torthowald in 1584. Johnstone himself was taken prisoner in 1585 by Lord Maxwell and took possession of the Castle. This was probably part of the ongoing feud between the two families culminating with the battle of Dryfe Sands in 1593.

In 1596 the Castle was back in the hands of the Maxwells, yet by 1602 by royal decree of James VI the Castle was again in the hands of the Johnstones. In 1617 it was sold back to Sir William Douglas 1st Earl of Queensbury. The Castle was then held in the Douglas family until 1890, by which time it was in ruins.

Other Scottish Fortifications

Aikwood Tower
Aikwood Tower is situated just to the west of Selkirk. It's a four-storey sixteenth century tower house. A tower existed here as far back as 1455 prior to the Battle of Arkinholme. In the early sixteenth century it passed into the Scott family, who built the Tower we see today. The Tower passed into the Scotts of Harden, another branch of the same family in 1602. The Harden Scotts are forever linked, in border folklore, to the tale of Muckle Mouth Meg, whose descendant was Sir Walter Scott. Today Aikwood has been fully restored and is a local wedding venue.

Amisfield Tower
Built in the late sixteenth century, this is a three-storey tower house. Yet the tower we see today with its fine corbelling may have been built or modified from an earlier tower on the same site. As legend has it James V visited Amisfield in 1530 on behalf of a widow who didn't get the support of the local laird. Sir John Charteris had the Tower built after he had succeeded to his father's lands in 1577 and served as Provost for James VI. The Tower is in good condition and measures thirty-one feet by twenty-eight and to a height of seventy-seven feet. The stair turret with a bartizan is of a unique design. The lower floor, in keeping with most tower houses, has a vaulted ceiling.

Ayton Castle
Situated nine miles north-west of Berwick on the outskirts of the village of Ayton, the neoclassical mansion seen today was built around an original fifteenth century tower house. The Castle was the stronghold of the Home family, who held sway in the Scottish East March during the fifteenth and sixteenth centuries. Very little, if anything, is left of the original tower house, as it was burnt down.

In 1497 the Castle was taken by the forces of the Earl of Surrey on his way to meet the forces of James IV and Perkin Warbeck, pretender to the English throne. Later in the same year it was the setting for the signing of the "Treaty of Ayton" between England and Scotland. Today the Castle is a hotel which uses the mansion, constructed in the nineteenth century.

Blackhouse Tower

Positioned just off the Southern Upland Way and just north of St Mary's Loch and Dryhope Tower is Blackhouse Tower. Today it is a ruin sitting on the left bank of the Douglas Burn. Based on an oblong plan and measuring twenty-five feet by thirty-one feet, with a circular stair tower in the south-west corner. The area is synonymous with the Douglas family and more specifically the Good Sir James Douglas, supporter of Robert the Bruce, who after raiding into England earned the nickname the Black Douglas. The Tower itself is of a later build, in all probability, from the late fifteenth century and early sixteenth century, when it was held by the Stewart family.

Blanerne Castle

Thought to be built around 1540 on the banks of the River Whiteadder, its remains are in the grounds of Blanerne House near Chirnside. There are two buildings in ruins, the keep and the guardhouse. They were once thought to be connected together. The guardhouse was originally being three-storeys high and measuring sixteen feet by sixteen feet. the remains stand thirty-f-seven feet high. The keep, being in a more ruinous state, measures sixteen feet by twenty-four feet.

The Castle was the seat of the Lumsdaine family for over four centuries. Blanerne house was built during the eighteenth century after the Castle had fallen into disrepair.

Branxholme Castle

A stronghold of the Scott family since the fifteenth century, this castle at Branxholme is just off the A7 south of Hawick. The Castle has been modified extensively over the centuries into more of a manor house. The Percys burned the castle in 1532 in a raid on Scotland. The original tower house consisted of five storeys and has a vaulted ceiling in the basement, where they would have stored cattle during a raid. In 1570 the Earl of Essex's English army attacked the Castle with gunpowder. The rebuilding was started by the 5th Duke of Buccleuch in 1837.

Bunkle Castle

Often referred to as Bonkyll Castle, it is situated near Blanerne Castle and close to the village of Preston. Little remains of the Castle today except for the motte or mound it stood on. The Castle had numerous owners though its lifetime starting with the Bonkyll family who built it in the thirteenth century, before becoming the property of the Home family who acquired it in the fifteenth century.

Comlongon Castle

The present Castle at Comlongon was built by Sir John Murray of Cockpool, after the rising at Lochmaben in 1493. It stands on the site of an earlier fortification, dating back to the thirteenth century. The Murrays had held the lands of Cockpool for 200 years, pre-dating their participation in the Battle of Otterburn in 1388. In 1570 Lady Marion Carruthers committed suicide by jumping from the lookout tower of the Castle, it is said her ghost haunts the Castle to this day. The castle is situated fifteen miles west of Gretna and nine miles east of Dumfries, near the village of Clarencefield. Comlongon has been refurbished and is now a prime wedding venue in the Scottish borders.

Corsbie Tower

Corsbie Tower was the property of the Cranstoun family, although very little now remains of what was an impressive fifty foot high tower house. Built to an oblong plan forty feet by twenty-seven feet with walls averaging six feet thick. The Tower collapsed sometime after 1955 when it was thought to be still almost complete.

Built on a raised piece of ground or motte, surrounded by a bog, the castle or tower used the bog as the first line of its defence. There is a double ditch system with inner and outer ditches. These were either side of what would have been a barmkin wall. The main approach to the Tower was from the north, via a causeway.

Cockburn Tower

One of the towers held by the Cockburn family, situated near the village of Cockburn in Berwickshire, the remains stand on a headland overlooking the Whiteadder Water. The Tower was built on an oblong plan with the remains measuring forty feet by thirty-seven feet and with walls nine feet thick. The Tower was built and controlled by the Dunbar family, probably built around the 1400s. The land was bought by William Cockburn from the Earl of Crawford in 1527; it remained the family seat of the Cockburn's until 1698. When the tower and the surrounding land were auctioned off to clear debts accrued by Sir James Cockburn, 1st Baronet. The Tower was not used as a residence and soon fell into disrepair, prior to the farm being constructed in 1820.

Fourmerkland Tower

Built in the late sixteenth century by Robert Maxwell, the foundations of this Tower are known to be older and most probably it was built on top of an existing tower. This is a traditional Scottish tower house with prominent bartizans, which are mounted on the north-east and south-west corners of the Tower. The house has a vaulted basement and originally had a barmkin and outbuildings, however there is no trace of them today. It is a three-storey building measuring twenty-four feet by nineteen feet and with walls that are three feet thick. Maxwells' crest is on a panel that is above the entrance to the Tower. This was occupied until 1790, to be restored in 1964 and today it remains unoccupied. It is not open to the general public and permission to view the Tower has to be obtained from Fourmerkland Farm.

Hoddom Castle

Hoddom Castle is situated about three miles from Ecclefechan in Dumfries and Galloway. The Castle was built by the Herries family who were supporters of the Bruce family who at the time were the Lords of Annandale. The Castle was then held by the Carruthers and the Maxwells who held the position of Warden of the West March. The Maxwells extended the Castle into the structure we see today. The Maxwells also had Repentance Tower built, on a hill to the south of the Castle, most likely as a watchtower. The Castle was captured in 1569 by supporters of Mary Queen of Scots. It was later attacked by the English army under Lord Scrope. Today the Castle resides within a caravan park and is in private hands.

Horsburgh Castle

Situated just off the A72 road from Peebles to Galashiels, the Castle today is just a ruin with a few walls left standing. It stands high above the River Tweed as it flows to the sea at Berwick. The Horsburgh family built the Castle around the 1470s and held it until the twentieth century; the family also built the Castle at Nether Horsburgh. Very little is known about the history of the Castle or any raids it may have sustained.

Lockerbie Tower

Lockerbie Tower is often known as Mains Tower or "the Mains", in all probability built by the Johnstones around the middle of the sixteenth century. One of a number of Johnstone towers in the area, it is built to an oblong plan, and measuring twenty-five feet by twenty feet. The Tower was originally positioned near two lochs, however these have been drained as the town of Lockerbie has grown and the Tower resided beside the police station until it was finally demolished in 1967.

Mangerton Tower

Mangerton was the tower and base of Thomas Armstrong. Thomas was the hedesman of the large Armstrong family during the sixteenth century. Mangerton is situated near the village of Newcastleton, formerly known as Copshaw Holm in the Scottish side of the Debateable Lands. The Tower today doesn't display the power it once held, being reduced to the lower walls of the first floor of what was originally a three-storey tower house similar in construction to Gilnockie a few miles away. Mangerton and the area are thought to have been in the Armstrong family from 1378 until it was given to Francis Scott in 1629. On one of the remaining walls is carved SA and EE, the initials of Simon (Sym) Armstrong and Elizabeth Elliot his wife. It is possible via a pleasant walk from the village to see the remains of Mangerton, beside the Liddel Water.

Nether Horsburgh Castle
Almost the twin castle of Horsburgh Castle, Nether Horsburgh lies a little further south on the A72 and on the opposite side of the road. The Castle is a small oblong measuring around thirty-two feet by twenty-six feet and with walls around four feet thick. In its prime there were probably four storeys. Today sadly it's just a ruin with the outer walls standing. There is evidence of the Castle having an outer barmkin.

Newark Castle
This five-storey tower house is situated in the grounds of Bowhill House just west of Selkirk. It was built or first mentioned in 1423 as the "New Werk" or Newark, built for Archibald Douglas. The tower passed to the possession of the Scottish crown and James II after the defeat of the Douglases at Arkinholme in 1455. In 1473 it passed to Margaret of Denmark, wife of James III. Besieged in 1547 by Lord Gray of Wilton, it was then burned by English forces in 1548. The Tower was then taken by Cromwellian forces in 1650 during the Civil War. The tower is of a rectangular design being sixty-four feet by fourty feet, originally having an outer barmkin. Today it is part of the Buccleuch estates and not open to the public, but can be seen from the road.

Old Thirlestane Castle
The tower sits above the Boondriegh Water, east of the village of Lauder. Built by Sir Richard Maitland around the mid thirteenth century, the Castle was held by the Maitland family until around 1595. The tower is built on an oblong plan, measuring thirty-three feet by twenty-four feet and with walls four feet thick.

The first floor was vaulted and used for keeping cattle during the frequent raids in the area in the reiving season. There is evidence of a barmkin around the remains of the tower keep.

The Raid and Capture of Geordie Burns
"The Confessions of a Reiver"

The Constables tower of Berwick Castle, although not held in this tower Geordie Burns was held in Berwick Castle

The Burns family were well known reivers from Teviotdale, in the Scottish Middle March. Allied often with the Ker family, they would join together in raids to Redesdale and Tynedale.

On the night of Monday 13 September 1596, Geordie Burns his uncle and two other members of the Burns family started out on a raid into the English East March, with the intention of lifting cattle, sheep and insight (household goods), most probably on the instructions of Robert Ker of Cessford. They travelled south without problem and lifted a good head of sheep. After midnight they travelled back towards Teviotdale.

The merry band of reivers were caught by surprise by a patrol commanded by Lord Hunsdon and observed by Sir Robert Carey, then the deputy warden of the English Middle March. The patrol attempted to retrieve the sheep and other goods from the Reivers. Two of the Burnses were killed in the ensuing fight, including Geordie Burns' uncle. One escaped into the black of the night, Geordie Burns himself was captured after sustaining a blow to the head and escorted to Berwick prison the next morning.

In most cases the offender would be hanged immediately or after a short trial and no more would be heard of them. However, what make this case different is the next thirty-six hours. Burns went on trial on the morning of 14 September accused of March Treason, to which he was found guilty and sentenced to death. March Treason was in effect a cover all for offences. The term March Treason means to betray the border, or march, to the enemy. The garrison at Berwick persuaded Carey to wait twenty-four hours before hanging Burns, to see if Robert Ker of Cessford would come for Burns, in order to set him free as had been done with Kinmont Willie at Carlisle. Carey agreed and Burns was placed back in the cells to await his fate. On the evening of 15 September Sir Robert Carey, dressed as a servant and with two of his soldiers, visited Burns in his cell in Berwick. He found Burns in a talkative and repentant mood, confessing to his crimes, including the murders of seven men, the sleeping with over forty other men's wives as well as other reiving crimes. Carey then noted these in his memoirs. On the 16 September Geordie Burns was hanged, in the early morning; however Sir Robert Carey's memoirs ensured that Geordie Burns has been remembered more than most.

Hobbie Noble
"An English Reiver amongst the Armstrongs"

The remains of Crew Castle today, it is listed as a castle but it is actually a Bastle house.

This tale disproves the suggestion that the reivers only made raids across the English-Scottish Border and that they didn't raid or steal from their own side. The tale also proves that the raiding was done by all classes of society. Born in Crew Castle in Bewcastle dale to the east of Cumberland, Hobbie was from a family that was better off than most. Born somewhere around the middle of the sixteenth century at the height of reiving times, it appears that Hobbie liked to reive and raid more than most. With this came violence, in a violent time, something we are led to believe Hobbie was good at.

If we trust Sir Walter Scott then the name Hobbie is derived from Halbert, others say that it is a mispronunciation of Robbie or Robert which appears more likely as it was a popular name in the borders. Whichever it was, throughout history and the ballads written about him and his misdeeds, he has been known as Hobbie Noble. The Noble family are well enough known as a reiving family to the west of Northumberland and the waste of what was then Cumberland.

Hobbie, it would appear, favoured raiding in Tynedale in Northumberland and other parts of Cumberland than across the Scottish border. Why this is we shall never know. What we do know is that the raids were frequent and violent and the people of Tynedale and the area surrounding Crew Castle in Bewcastle area really got fed up with Hobbie and his followers. They ganged up against Hobbie and "put him to the horn" which meant they drove him out of Crew Castle and Bewcastle to the Debateable Lands of Liddesdale into the hands of the Armstrongs where a lot of the broken men resided.

The Armstrong family were well known as reivers and had their power base at Mangerton near what was Copshaw Holm, now better known as Newcastleton in the Debateable Lands. Here Hobbie was befriended as a fellow reiver by the Laird of Mangerton. From here Hobbie went on raids to other areas of the Scottish borders, however not to the area of either Tyndale or Bewcastle as both the Warden of the West March and the Land Sergeant at Askerton wanted Hobbie for March Treason. Indeed Hobbie was well received by the Armstrongs in particular, after one raid to rescue one of their own from Newcastle.

Jock o' the Side was thought to be the Laird of Mangerton's nephew so he was well connected and thought of within the Armstrong family. He was also a noted reiver and during a raid into Northumberland with his companions was caught by the patrol. Some of the party were killed after a fight and Jock was captured and taken to Newcastle and gaoled in the Castle. This meant certain execution for Jock at the end of the rope after what would probably be a short trial.

Together with The Lairds Jock (The Laird's son John) and the Lairds Wat (The Laird's son Walter) Hobbie planned the release of Jock from Newcastle. It is said that they set off from Liddesdale, skirting the Bewcastle area, on a foul night with driving rain. They reached Newcastle but couldn't find an open door or other easy way in, as the ladder that they brought with them was too short. Finding a guard station they managed to overpower and kill the guard, after a fight. They then found Jock, in chains, and carried him to his horse. They set off for Liddesdale with Jock still in chains. It is believed they crossed the Tyne, which was swollen, near to Chollerford, after which they stopped to remove the chains from Jock, before continuing their journey to Liddesdale.

This put Hobbie in great stead with the Laird and most of his family, however some of the Armstrong family resented Hobbie and the favour in which he was held. Notable to this was Simon Armstrong of Main near Castletoun, often known as Sym of the Mains. Sym wanted to see the downfall of this English reiver and so plotted against him. To do this Sym persuaded Hobbie to lead a raid (probably against his better judgement) into England and dangerous territory for Hobbie.

As Hobbie led the party including Sym south via Kershope Burn into England. Sym had sent word to the Land Sergeant at Askerton of the details of the raid and the route to be taken. The raid would mean an overnight rest at this point but when Hobbie awoke, the next morning, instead of finding Sym and the rest of the Armstrong party; he looked into the faces of the English warden's men. Hobbie was tied with his own bowstring and led, in disgrace, to Carlisle Castle dungeons.

While in the dungeons Hobbie was told to confess to stealing a horse from Peter of Winfield in order to spare his life. Hobbie refused this offer and was hanged the next morning on Harabee Hill just outside Carlisle Castle. The betrayal of Hobbie reached the ears of the Laird of Mangerton, who was furious.

The laird vowed retribution at the betrayal of Hobbie and, as such, a few months later another raid into England took place, led by Sym o' the Mains, this time the English wardens were ready again, furnished with information supplied by Mangerton. Sym was duly captured and after a night in the cells was hung the next morning on Harabee Hill, closing this sad tale of betrayal and retribution.

Johnnie Armstrong
"Murder at the Hands of a King"

In the early part of the sixteenth century Johnnie Armstrong, or Johnnie of Gilnockie as he was better known, a reference to the tower house he lived in on the banks of the River Esk, was very popular with his followers but naturally not so with his enemies south of the Border. He raided on both sides of the Border, upsetting the locals and both the realms of England and Scotland which would eventually lead to his sad demise. As the youngest son of the Laird of Mangerton, Johnnie held a considerable amount of power in the borders. Since he was married to Elizabeth Graham in the early 1520s, it allied Johnnie with the equally large and notorious Graham clan giving him alliances on both sides of the Border. To Johnnie, blackmail, extortion, reiving and piracy were second nature making him a wealthy man. This wealth and power made him an embarrassment to the Scottish crown and to others in the area who would be glad to see his downfall.

When James V of Scotland came to rule in his own right the borders were in disarray. Encouraged by his English counterpart Henry VIII, James decided that something must be done about them. In 1530 he rode out of Edinburgh with a large force determined to bring the Borders into line. On the way south they had some success and some reivers were captured and sent back to Edinburgh for trial and execution. Then James and his party reached Caerlenrigg where they camped and decided to rest and do some hunting in the Ettrick Forrest.

The King sent a message to Johnnie and his followers to meet him at or in Caerlenrigg for some hunting and talks, assuring Johnnie of safe passage. The invitation pleased Johnnie who accepted without any fears for his safety. On the appointed day Johnnie and his followers, thought to be about thirty-six men dressed in their finery, and it is thought that they were unarmed, proceeded north to Caerlenrigg. They set off not from Gilnockie but from Langholm Castle where Johnnie had been staying. Whilst travelling through the area known as Mosspaul, a narrow passage near the present day A7, they were confronted by an advance party of some of the *King's followers and escorted to Caerlenrigg.*

The Johnnie Armstrong plaque at Carlenrig church yard.

Arriving at Caerlenrigg Johnnie and his followers were taken straight to the King whereupon, seeing that Johnnie was better dressed than he was, the King changed his mood. The mood darkened and it became apparent to Johnnie that his life and that of his followers was in danger. Being a typical reiver and silver tongued, Johnnie tried to talk himself out of the situation. When this failed, he then tried to bribe the King with assurances that he had never harmed a fellow Scot and that all south of the Border to the River Tyne would pay homage to him and, therefore, to the King.

The field at Carlenrig at Teviothead, the stone marks the grave of Johnnie Armstrong and his followers.

The promises fell on deaf ears and the King ordered the executions. In one final act of defiance, mocking James, Johnnie said these words:

"I am but a fool to seek grace at a graceless face, but had I known you would have taken me this day, I would have lived in the borders despite King Harry and you both." The reference to King Harry meant Henry VIII.

Johnnie Armstrong and all his men were then taken out and hung from the nearby trees. They were all buried together in a mass grave, where today a stone stands on the spot where the graves were found, against the churchyard wall there is a plaque dedicated to Johnnie and his men. In certain quarters Johnnie despite been being a bandit and a thug, was exceedingly popular and has gone down as a bit of a borders Robin Hood-type character.

There is no record of any trial being conducted either in English or Scottish annals. The King handing out his own Jeddart Justice (hang first and ask questions later). The act of hanging sent shockwaves through the borders and, far from bringing them into line, it alienated most of the local families against the King, even if they didn't like Johnnie or the Armstrongs. They had fought against one another many times and had even had blood feuds but the families in the borders considered this act by the King as underhanded and extremely unjust, not what they would expect from their monarch.

The Rescue of Kinmont Willie
April 16th 1596

Kershopfoot or Tourneyholm, it was on his way from here after a Truce day that Kinmont was captured.

William Armstrong of Kinmont, more often known as Kinmont Willie, had his base and tower at Morton Rigg, just north of Carlisle. A noted reiver with a large following known as "Kinmont's Bairns", who were in effect robbers, plunderers and cattle thieves par excellence. They raided both England and Scotland with equal regularity, the larger the raid the more they were likely to be involved.

With truce days a regular occurrence in the borders for the wardens to sort out trials and other cross -order business, this day gave safe passage to all involved until sun up the next day. A truce day being called for on 17 March 1596, to be held at Kershopfoot just over the Scottish Border (a common place for meeting), Kinmont Willie attended the meeting on behalf of Scott of Buccleugh for the Scottish side. Kinmont having a large number of family both in the Debatable Lands and in Scotland, at the time held the office of "the Keeper of Liddesdale".

The day itself, we presume, passed without incident as nothing of note is reported. After the day's events Kinmont made his way back to his tower in Morton Rigg alone. A group of Englishmen, presumably who had also been at the earlier events, spotted Kinmont riding alone and after a brief chase they succeeded in capturing him and then escorting him to Carlisle Castle, giving delight to Lord Scrope (the younger) Warden of the English West March. Yet the capture of Kinmont on this day was in clear breach of the rules of a day of truce enraged the Scottish side, in particular Scott of Buccleugh. Scott vowed to release Kinmont at the earliest opportunity.

A plot to release Kinmont was hatched by Buccleugh, it is said at either a game of football or a race meeting. The attempt would include four of Kinmont's own sons and a number of other reivers having close links to Kinmont or Buccleugh. Accounts vary about the number, from twenty to eighty, but it is likely that it is nearer the lower figure. The group included Scotts, Armstrongs and Grahams, Kinmont being married to Huchin Graham's daughter.

On the night of the 13 April 1596 the party set out to rescue Kinmont from the Scottish side of the Border. The night was dark and with heavy rain, not the best for riding, let alone a rescue of a prisoner in a heavily guarded castle. They had to ride through the Debateable Lands and then cross the River Eden, in full spate at the time, in a place where they couldn't be seen from the Castle. They carried with them a ladder to reach a small postern gate on the west wall; it is thought that Buccleugh, through the Grahams, who had both family and associates working within the Castle staff, had bribed a member of the Castle staff to leave this gate open.

Entering the Castle they searched for Kinmont in the cell block, harming no one else except a couple of the Castle guards and with the only thought of rescuing Kinmont. When they found Kinmont in shackles languishing in the cells, Scrope had intended to hang Kinmont the next morning, the 14 April for March Treason, they carried Kinmont down the ladder to the rest of the party waiting with the ponies and made off towards the Scottish Border, pursued by a large contingent of the Castle garrison said to be over 1,000 men. The escape party had a head start and only stopped when they had crossed the Border into Scotland. They then released Kinmont from his metal restraints.

The postern or service gate at Carlisle Castle where the rescuers took Kinmont Willie through to freedom.

The escape of Kinmont from under the noses of the garrison at Carlisle had ramifications on both sides of the Border. King James VI worried that it might affect his wish to succeed Queen Elizabeth to the throne of England. Queen Elizabeth was deeply annoyed at the embarrassment of a noted border reiver escaping from one of the strongholds of the borders.

Scrope, having pursued the party into Scotland, was rightly highly embarrassed and would have to answer to Queen Elizabeth, in his capacity as Warden of the English East March. He vented his anger by burning the towns of Dumfries and Annan, capturing nearly 200 people. He marched them back to Carlisle, barefoot. That only fanned the flames of the English embarrassment, with the Queen now venting her anger on Scrope.

After Scrope's first assessment to the Queen, and attempt at admonishing himself from blame for the incident, fell wide of the mark, he resorted in blaming his subordinates in the Lowthers and the Carletons both of whom had dealings with the Scottish reivers and had relatives married to the Grahams.

Meanwhile north of the Border King James, angered at the involvement of Buccleugh, ordered him to surrender himself to the English. Although, all things considered, the actions of Buccleugh were both daring and bold, indeed after this escapade he would be known as "the Bold Buccleugh". After something of an ambassadorial merry-go-round between the two sides Buccleugh was, eventually to be wardened in Berwick in October 1597, over a year after the raid.

As with most disputes the "Kinmont affair" started losing momentum and petered out. Kinmont himself laid low, for a while at least, before starting again at what he did best: reiving. Kinmont lived out his life, ultimately dying of old age at his tower in Morton Rigg, north of Carlisle, somewhere between 1603 and 1611, when exactly is undocumented.

Lang Sandy Armstrong
The Tall One is Hanged"

The statue of Lang Sandy at Rowanburn, his tower house was in the fields nearby.

In an age when the average height of a man was barely (just) over five feet, Alexander Armstrong of Rowenburn in the Debatable Lands stood at over six feet, earning him the nickname of Lang Sandy. Sandy lived in a tower house in the village of Rowenburn, but nothing unfortunately remains of the tower, it is rumoured that Lang Sandy, who was also known as Sandies Ringane, had eleven sons and was the brother of William Armstrong of Kinmont, more commonly called Kinmont Willie.

In 1600 Sir John Carmichael the Warden of the Scottish West March served notice on the reivers that he would be tough on any caught, even those on the Scottish side. The Armstrongs, knowing the directive would affect them more than most clans in the Border, asked for a meeting to resolve the issue and probably gain some leniency. For the meeting Sir John came with some of his deputies and a few hangers-on, Kinmont for his part sent his brother Sandy even though Sandy was an old man in 1600.

The meeting didn't go well, some of Sir John's companions started ridiculing Sandy. Then they cut his sword belt and put eggs in the scabbard to humiliate him, for once the sword was placed back in the scabbard it couldn't be withdrawn. This was seen as a jest by Carmichael's men but utter humiliation by the Armstrongs and they swore vengeance, in true Reiver fashion. The meeting did not end well with accusations on both sides.

Later that year, at a truce day, a football match was held. During the day Thomas Armstrong, Sandy's son, met with the Irvines and Scotts to start plotting the revenge of Lang Sandy. The result of the meeting was that Sir John would have to be removed from office; as this was unlikely to happen by either him resigning or being removed by the King, he would have to die.

In June of 1600 whilst Sir John Carmichael was on his way from Langholm to Lochmaben to preside over a warden court, he was ambushed by a party of Armstrongs that included Thomas Armstrong and his father Sandy, together with a Taylor, a Graham, a Scott and a Forrester. Carmichael was killed in the ambush, his death was lamented by the English West March Warden, Sir Richard Lowther. After the ambush the group then raided the area round Stanwix, removing cattle and horses.

After this the party scattered to avoid the searching party, King James VI was furious and ordered the search and pursuit of the party, who sought refuge with friends. The search took until the following year when Thomas Armstrong was caught and tried. Found guilty he was taken to Edinburgh where his right hand was cut off, he was then hanged at the Mercat Cross. His body was then strung up in chains for all to see.

Lang Sandy evaded capture until 1606. When he was caught, he admitted his part in the ambush saying he was forced into resorting to violence. Lang Sandy was hanged along with all eleven of his sons; this bringing to a close the murder of Sir John Carmichael.

Today there is a statue in the village of Rowenburn to Lang Sandy.

The Tale of Muckle Mouth Meg
"The Hangman or a Wife"

Elibank Castle, home of Sir Gideon Murray

Walter Scott of Harden, a noted reiver, known more commonly as Auld Wat of Harden and a descendant of Sir Walter Scott who famously said as he passed by a hay bale "if ye had fower legs then ye wouldnae bide there lang" he also participated in the rescue of Kinmont Willie from Carlisle Castle. Auld Wat married Mary, the flower of Yarrow, a noted beauty of the time. Together they had seven sons all brought up in great reiver tradition. If it wasn't too hot or too heavy it could be carried off. The oldest of the sons, Will Scott, took full advantage of this and caused quite a stir in the process.

Whilst out reiving near to home at Elibank young Will got caught by none other than Sir Gideon Murray of Elibank, whose cattle young Will was busy lifting. The penalty for reiving cattle at the time was death, by hanging, and in most cases this would have been sudden and quickly done, often from the nearest tree on the same day without trial. However young Will was nothing if not lucky as he was placed in Sir Gideon's cells overnight with the promise that he would be hung next day, Sir Gideon even sent out invitations for the hanging.

The statue to Meg and Will Scott at Thornliebank in Tweedale, not far from Elibank Castle.

The good Lady Murray, having seen the handsome young chap languishing in the dungeons, had other ideas. You see the Murrays had daughters and one in particular was giving them cause for concern. Not the prettiest girl around, indeed her mouth was her most notable feature was Lady Agnes Murray, to give the young lady her proper name. However history would know her as Muckle Mouth Meg. She was quite plain looking, rather than being particularly ugly, as history has stated.

Having failed to find a suitable husband the Murrays were resigned to having their daughter with them throughout their lives. With young Will contemplating his fate with the hangman next day. Lady Murray pleaded with her husband to exchange Will's life for the chance to marry Lady Agnes instead. Eventually Sir Gideon relented to his wife's more sensible suggestion and the proposition was then put to the hapless Will, who asked for time to consider it.

Three times young Will almost chose the noose over Meg, but when almost at the gallows tree, there stood Meg with arms open. A final change of heart by the young lad saw him shake loose from his captors and fall into the grateful and loving arms of Lady Agnes. Indeed a very short time later the young couple were married, the union was a long and loving one, six generations later Sir Walter Scott was born into this family. The tale was immortalised by James Hogg "the Ettrick Shepherd" a close friend of Sir Walter Scott in "the fray of Elibank".

It is interesting to note that the marriage contract for young Will and Meg is quite long, at 102 inches in length.

Richie Graham
"The Blackmailer Extraordinaire"

Harbottle Castle where Sir John Forster had his first command.

Whoever said "crime doesn't pay" has obviously never heard about the blackmailer and reiver Richie Graham of Brackenhill. Richie was born around 1555 in the north of Cumberland bordering on the Debatable Lands, he was the son of Fergus Graham of Mote. Richard, or Richie Graham as he is better documented lived at a time when anarchy ruled the borders between England and Scotland and the state law was well disregarded by the vast majority of the reiving fraternity of which the Grahams were a prominent family.

Comparatively little is known about him until 1584 when he was indicted for the murder of George Graham, more commonly known as Parcivalls Geordie at Levens Bridge. Richie and an accomplice stabbed poor Geordie and left him, who died three weeks later in Carlisle. As far as is known Richie never stood trial for this murder. It's unusual that a case of murder in the borders between two people of the same family name is recorded, so much for loyalty within the family.

The year 1584 is also the year, it is thought, that Richie built the tower at Brackenhill; again it's unusual as it is in the Scottish vernacular style and is possibly the only one of its type on the English side of the Border. All the others of that style are on the Scottish side. He was also a man that could turn his hand to many things as well as murder, none of them however being on the right side of the law as far as we know it. These include counterfeiting, horse stealing, blackmail and conspiracy and getting away with all his crimes as nowhere is he seen to be convicted of any of them. For Thomas, Lord Scrope, the English Warden of the West March, Richie proved to be a large thorn in the side, a bit like an itch he couldn't scratch.

Aurthuret Church near Longtown, where Richie Graham used to post the notices on the door of the church.

Let's look at Richie's blackmailing, the area where he gained his notoriety. He must have been supremely confident against the authorities when going around collecting his blackmail. It's said that he would pin a list of those owing him money on the door of Arthuret Church. Some even say that the list was pinned up with a dagger in case anyone should have any doubts about not paying. On occasion he would sit in the entrance to the church and collect the money himself. Richie would blackmail the local farmers around the Brackenhill area, saying that he could protect them from the Reivers. This was a form of a protection racket. It is of course impossible for Richie to be everywhere and protect the good people of north Cumberland; they in fact were only paying to be protected from Richie and his henchmen the main one of these was one Thomas "the Merchant" Hetherington who kept the books for Richie.

Richie's blackmailing was so well entrenched in the local area that when one Gilsland resident went to complain about paying his 'black, rent to Richie and his 'green' or normal rent to the Crown, he found Richie in a local pub with none other than the Land Sergeant of Gilsland one Thomas Carleton (quite well known for his double dealing).

Well known in the borders as a horse thief, Richie didn't bother too much who he stole them from. Indeed it is said that one raid on Falkland Palace netted Richie eighty good horses. There were raids on Falkland Palace during this period, notably one with the Earl of Bothwell trying to capture the King. The raid could easily have been the same one that Richie Graham got his horses from, as Francis Stewart the Earl of Bothwell did use reivers both English and Scottish on this raid.

The raid to rescue Kinmont Willie involved the Grahams and in particular Richie, as a conspirator to the bribing of people inside Carlisle Castle, so that the Scots rescue party could get safe passage. Richie probably saw the assistance as "getting one over" on the West March Warden Thomas, Lord Scrope.

Eventually Richie was hauled before the Privy Council to answer for his misdeeds, including conspiracy, murder and reiving. Somehow Richie escaped without punishment. Possibly the reason is that, at the time, relations between England and

Scotland were not at their best and the Grahams were keeping the Scots otherwise occupied.

Nothing is known of the whereabouts of Richie Graham after the Privy Council inquisition of 1600. It is presumed that he died of old age after the turn of the century.

Sir John Carmichael
(1542-1600)
"A better Englishman than a Scotsman"

Mosspaul today is a very tranquil place, but it isn't hard to picture how the Armstrongs would have ambushed Sir John Carmichael.

The tribute given to Sir John on his death by King James VI gives some indication of the man. Descended from the Earls of Hindford (or Hyndford) and born into a formidable Lanarkshire family, John Carmichael rose to become one of the most respected march wardens on the borders and Keeper of Liddesdale during a very turbulent time.

Sir John was born in 1542 in Lanarkshire son of John Carmichael and Elizabeth, the daughter of the 5th Lord Somerville. Little if anything is known about his early life until the Raid of the Redeswire in 1575.

At the Redeswire he served as the deputy march warden of the Scottish Middle March. He presided over the truce day at Carter Bar opposite Sir John Forster the Warden of the English Middle March. The day did not go well and after accusations from both sides it descended into an affray and a subsequent political row between England and Scotland as to what started the affray.

For his part in the affray, Sir John was wardened in York in an effort to get to the truth and appease the English Crown. He was released to go back to the borders later that year.

Lochmaben castle, where Sir John Carmichael was destined before being ambushed by the Armstrongs.

Sir John too part in the Raid of Ruthven in 1582, together with his son Hugh and William Carmichael of Rowantreecross, they fought for King James VI and after the King's defeat and capture, Sir John was arrested in 1584 and forfeited lands. The Raid was actually the daring capture of the young James VI of Scotland and they held him captive for a while to delay the return of his mother, Mary Queen of Scots back to Scotland and the reinstatement of the Catholic Church. It is obvious that Sir John was at this time in contact with the King as the forfeiture didn't last long and the lands were soon restored. Not only that, the King sent Sir John as an ambassador to Denmark to negotiate the

King's own marriage to Anne of Denmark, daughter of the Danish King.

Sir John was knighted at the coronation of Queen Anne (Anne of Denmark, Queen to King James VI) on the 15 May 1590. In 1592 he resigned the wardenship of the Scottish West March in favour of the Earl of Angus. In 1598 Sir John resumed the wardenship of the West March from the Earl of Angus, vowing to take to task the border reivers.

The wardenship brought him into conflict with a number of the large border families in particular the Armstrongs of Liddesdale; this would lead to his downfall. In a meeting with some Armstrongs, some of Sir John's followers mocked the elderly Armstrong the brother of Kinmont Willie Armstrong, who swore revenge. Whilst travelling from Langholm to Lochmaben for a warden court in 1600, Sir John was attacked and killed by a group of Armstrongs. All the culprits were caught and hanged by order of King James VI, who was much saddened by the death of Sir John Carmichael.

Sir John Forster
(1502-1602)
"The Old Rogue"

Often called "that old rogue" Sir John lived to be around 100 years old, a remarkable feat in Elizabethan times. Sir John Forster was born around 1502 although some say he was born as late as 1527, the second son of Sir Thomas Forster of Etherston in Northumberland and Dorothy Ogle, daughter of Ralph Ogle and Margaret Gascoigne. Sir John was born at Adderstone near Bamburgh at a time when his father was Marshall of Berwick.

Schooled from an early age in warfare and politics of the borders, Sir John would become well known for his wheeling and dealing throughout the borders. During 1542 he fought at the Battle of Solway Moss, a decisive English victory in the English West March, though there is some conjecture as to whether or not he captured Robert Maxwell, the 5th Lord Maxwell and noted Scottish Warden of the West March. In the same year he was charged with the captaincy of Harbottle Castle and its garrison, thought to be of 100 men.

He fought with Somerset, the Lord Protector of England, at the Battle of Pinkie Cleugh against the Scots after which he was knighted by Somerset. Sir John was then given the position of Sheriff of Northumberland from 1549-1550. This brought its own financial rewards for Sir John and he accumulated more lands in northern Northumberland. Later in Edward VI's reign probably around 1555 he was awarded the captaincy of Bamburgh Garrison.

He married Jane, the daughter of Cuthbert Radcliffe and Margaret De Clifford in 1552, with whom he had several daughters. His son Thomas was born out of wedlock by Isobel Sheppard, who he married in 1568. Noted for caring and treating his servants well, he liked their families to be well presented.

At the siege of Berwick in 1560, under the Duke of Norfolk, he commanded a section of light cavalry, most probably border prickers. Following this in 1563 he was made deputy Warden of the English East March, based in Berwick, being one of only a few local born English wardens to serve in the borders.

During the rising of the northern barons in 1569, he fought for Elizabeth to repress the uprising of the Earls of Westmorland and Northumberland who wanted to re-establish Catholicism on the throne of England. Indeed it was Sir John who received the order to execute the captured Earl of Northumberland in 1572.

At the Redeswire on the 7 July 1575 Sir John was due to preside for the English side, with Sir John Carmichael presiding for the Scottish cause. Whilst the day started amiably it deteriorated when Sir John Forster didn't produce a noted English reiver to answer for his crimes. The argument quickly turned into an affray and during the affray Sir John Forster was captured and taken to Jedburgh. Sir George Heron of Chipchase, his deputy that day, was killed in the affray, which was ultimately won by the Scots. After remonstrations by Queen Elizabeth he was immediately released.

On 24th July 1585 Sir John was out riding with his son-in-law Lord Francis Russell. They were attacked by a party of Kerrs from Ferniehirst led by Sir Thomas Kerr of Ferniehirst. The Lord Russell was killed but Sir John escaped, later passing the action off as an accident. The English government didn't like this description of the event, describing it as a plot.

In 1588 a tramp was found wandering in the borders by men under the command of Sir John, on closer scrutiny the man didn't fit the pattern of men who wandered around at that time. Sir John searched the items the man had on him which appeared to be those used by dentists of the time. Within the dentistry equipment was a small mirror, and close scrutiny of the mirror revealed a letter hidden inside. The letter didn't make much sense to Sir John or any of his men. Rather than throw the letter away he sent it to Sir Francis Walmsley in London, Queen Elizabeth's spymaster. Sir Francis had the letter decoded and it revealed the outline plans for what we now know as the Spanish Armada. Using his spies Sir Francis was able to gain valuable information on the strength of the Armada before it sailed, all because of the capture of a wandering dentist in the borders.

Accusations at this time abounded against Sir John for his corruption and double dealing so he was relieved of his duties as warden. These accusations were outlined on 27 September 1586, where upon Sir John was dismissed from office. The accusations were then presented to Lord Hunsdon, who dismissed the charges and reinstated Sir John to the wardenry in 1588 where he served until 1595 when a combination of old age and further accusations resulted in him being removed from office.

Sir John retired to the village of Bamburgh. On 24 October 1597 a party of Scots rode to Bamburgh to settle old scores with Sir John. At the last minute Lady Forster managed to lock the door and the raiders went away. He died at Bamburgh on 13 January, 1602

Sir Robert Carey
(1560-1639)
"The Courtier"

Tarras Moss today on the outskirts of the village of Canonbie, during reiving times it was a large bog within the debateable lands.

Sir Robert Carey was probably one of the most enigmatic march wardens of the Anglo-Scottish Border during the sixteenth and early seventeenth centuries. He became a respected foe of many a reiver and was second cousin to Queen Elizabeth I.

Born in 1560 to Henry Carey, Lord Hunsdon and his wife Ann Morgan, Robert was the tenth and youngest of the Carey children. It is possible he was born near Berwick as his father was the East March Warden; if he wasn't born there then he certainly spent a part of his childhood in the area, developing a love for the area and its people. Taught by tutors at home, like so many of his status at that time, he profited little as the youngest in a large family.

At seventeen in 1577 he left England for Holland to become a member of Sir Thomas Layton's embassy in the Netherlands. Serving in the Netherlands until at least 1581, after which he returned to England and the Royal court (an environment he excelled in) he became noticed by the Queen. In 1587 he earned the Queen's favour when he persuaded the Earl of Essex another of the Queen's favourites not to go with the expedition to Sluys so that he could spend longer at the Queen's court.

When Mary, Queen of Scots was executed by Elizabeth in 1583, Carey was sent as an envoy to James VI to pacify the Scots. However on this first trip James wouldn't let Carey come any nearer to Scotland than Berwick. It wouldn't be the last time he would play this role and he later became known and trusted by James VI.

Carey enjoyed the good life and liked to gamble, and this pushed him into debt. As a result in 1589 he accepted a wager to walk from London to Berwick upon Tweed in twelve days. This was duly completed winning him the wager of £2,000, a considerable sum in those days. The wager showed a number of things that would stand him in good stead with the reivers later in life. He had a mental and physical strength, which they admired greatly and he liked to gamble, another trait which would serve him well in the borders.

During 1591 the Earl of Essex led an expedition to France and Carey joined him on the expedition. At some point Queen Elizabeth ordered the Earl to return to England. In a reverse of earlier persuasion Carey was sent to persuade the Queen that Essex did not have to return. This he achieved and no sooner had he done this, then he returned to France with Essex. He was then knighted by the Earl of Essex, in recognition of his service.

He was made the deputy Warden of the English West March in 1593, under his brother-in-law Lord Thomas Scrope (the younger Scrope), later that year he married Elizabeth Widdrington (née Trevanion), widow of Sir Henry Widdrington and Carey's first cousin. The Queen disapproved greatly of the marriage and for a time Carey was out of favour at the royal court. Later, in a gamble, on a visit to London he bought the Queen an expensive present (£400), this appeared to alleviate the tension and he was forgiven.

In 1595 he was made captain of Norham Castle in Northumberland, much to the dismay of his older brother John. This led to him being made Warden of the English East March stationed at Berwick-upon-Tweed in 1596. During this time he assisted in the Middle March and, during one of the patrols, they captured the reiver Geordie Burns. Carey had him taken to Berwick to be hung, on a charge of March Treason but, the night before the hanging, he went to see Burns disguised as a soldier. Burns made a full confession to him, which Carey documented in his memoirs.

Another time whilst Warden he decided to stake out the notorious Armstrong family who were living in an area called Tarras Moss in the Debatable Lands. He did this for a number of nights in the freezing cold. The story goes that the Armstrongs went out of the Moss by a different route on a raiding party and sent Carey a message with some beef so he could keep warm and be well fed, this beef is reported to be from Carey's own cows.

When Queen Elizabeth I was dying, in March 1603, Carey's sister Philadelphia, Lady Scrope was one of the Queen's Ladies of the Bedchamber. On the Queen's death she removed a ring from the Queen's finger (thought to be blue sapphire) and threw it out of a window to Carey. The ring had been given to Elizabeth by James VI and it is thought that it was to be returned to James when Elizabeth died, as proof of his ascension to the English throne.

Carey then rode for sixty hours solidly, using three horses and even falling off one and being kicked by the horse. He made good his promise to James that he would be the first with the news of the Queen's death. In recognition of this, Carey was made a Gentleman of the Scottish Bedchamber, however James later retracted this, after protests from London. Carey would eventually be given the title of Baron Leppington in 1622, this was in recognition of services to James's son Charles I. He was then made 1st Earl of Monmouth in 1625.

Carey died at Moor Park in Hertfordshire on 12 April 1639 and was buried at Rickmansworth, and not in Westminster Abbey as Carey himself had wanted and indicated in his will.

Sir Robert Ker
(1570-1650)
"The Fyrebrand"

Floors Castle in Roxburghshire, Home to the Dukes of Roxburghe as seen from the remains of Roxburghe Castle.

The noted reiver and Scottish politician was born in Cessford Castle Roxboroughshire in 1570, the eldest son of Sir William Ker and his wife Janet Douglas, the daughter of Sir James Douglas of Drumlanrig. Robert Ker was noted for his fiery and quick temper and, like most borderers on both sides at that times known to hold a grudge.

At the age of only seventeen in 1587 he married Margaret Maitland, the only daughter of Sir William Maitland of Lethington, the Secretary of State for Scotland under Mary of Guise and his second wife Mary Fleming (one of Mary, Queen of Scots' famed Four Marys).

During 1590 in a dispute with the Kers of Ferniehirst Sir Robert murdered Sir William Ker of Ancrum one night in

Edinburgh. This threw the two branches of the Kerr family into open conflict, with William's son, Sir Robert Ker vowing revenge as a blood feud. Sir Robert fled to England for a time but later in that year he returned to Scotland, under the protection of his uncle Sir John Maitland of Thirlistane. He was granted a pardon by James VI in order to raise support for the King against Francis Stewart the Earl of Bothwell. The next year Sir Robert received lands from the Crown that had been forfeited by Bothwell after the uprising.

In 1594 Sir Robert was given the job of the deputy Warden of the Scottish Middle March. This year also finds him having to raise troops again, with Lord Hume and the Laird of Buccleuch against another uprising by Francis Stewart. This time Stewarts Castle at Crichton was raised to the ground on royal orders. This help given to the King by Sir Robert further raised his standing at the royal court. Although he was the deputy March Warden there is no indication that he gave up the traditional border pastime of reiving, Glendale near Wooler in Northumberland being a particularly favourite area.

In 1596 Sir Robert Carey became Warden of the English East March based in Berwick; at the time Sir Robert Ker (Carey calls him Car in his memoirs and Anglicising of the name Ker) was warden of the Scottish middle march. In good faith, Carey sent a letter with a messenger to Ker asking if they could meet. Ker then plied the messenger with drink and set out that night to raid and reive the English East March. During the night's raiding Ker and his party killed one poor smallholder outside his house, for what would appear to be no other reason than that he was there. The party returned back to Cessford before the messenger awoke and wrote back to Carey a charming letter, omitting to tell him of the night's deeds. The deeds Carey later found out about from others, and they left him vowing to capture Ker and have him stand trial.

However things took a turn for the worst when Carey arrested Geordie Bourne in September 1596. Geordie was a favourite henchman of Sir Robert. Before Sir Robert could talk with Carey, Bourne had been hanged at Berwick. Sir Robert was annoyed about this and it started a feud between the two men. This came to a close two years later in 1598 when Sir Robert Ker was handed over as surety by another Scottish warden, Lord Hume.

Sir Robert chose Carey to be his guardian whilst in Berwick. Carey then housed Sir Robert in his own house and under the understanding he would not escape (a gentleman's handshake). Carey gave him the freedom to come and go as he pleased. This Sir Robert did and after a few days he sent for Carey to talk, the men settled their differences and according to Carey became firm friends. At least there is no recorded trouble between the two men after this point. Carey was ordered to deliver Sir Robert to York, which he duly did into the custody of the Archbishop. However, before June of 1598 Sir Robert was freed and back in Scotland.

Sir Robert was admitted to the Scottish Privy Council in 1599, a function he took seriously and attended regular meetings. In 1600 Sir Robert was raised to the peerage as Lord Roxburgh, this gave him various lands in the borders. When James VI travelled to England to claim and receive the English crown, Sir Robert travelled with him. He stayed in England until about 1606, apart from one visit to attend parliament in Edinburgh in 1604. At this parliament he was admitted to the Lords of the Articles, and became one of the commissioners to negotiate with England on Scotland's behalf.

He succeeded to his father's estates in 1606. In 1607 and in front of the Privy Council he settled his differences with Sir Robert Ker of Ancrum; this arose from the murder of Sir William Ker in 1590. It took several appearances before they agreed to settle their differences. Sir Robert apologised to the Ferniehirst Kers and paid them 10,000 merks (equivalent of £6,666 13s. 4d.)

The year of 1614 found Sir Robert widowed and he married Jean Drummond, daughter of Patrick, Lord Drummond and governess to the children of James VI at Somerset House. They had one child, a son Harry, born in 1618; unfortunately he would not outlive his father, dying in 1643 after a night of heavy drinking. For his political work in 1616, Sir Robert, was made the 1st Earl Roxburgh and gained the titles Lord Cessford and Caverton.

He continued his royal and political work on the accesssion of Charles I to the throne. Remaining in politics in the 1640s he supported the King in the Civil War, and due to this he was stripped of all parliamentary duties in 1648, although he was well into his seventies by then. Sir Robert died at his residence in

Floors (not the current Floors Castle) near Kelso on 18 January 1650. In his will he had secured special permission that his titles and lands go to his grandson William Drummond, on condition that he married his first cousin Jean Ker, the daughter of Sir Roberts's deceased son Harry. This he readily agreed to and changed his name to Ker; he became the 2nd Duke of Roxburgh.

Lord Bothwell and Wee Jock of the Park
"How to lose a castle"

James Bothwell the 6th Earl of Bothwell and lover of Mary, Queen of Scots was no lover of the reivers, and in particular the Elliotts. So it's no coincidence that in 1566 whilst Bothwell was the Keeper of Liddesdale and stationed in Hermitage Castle the two came together. It is said that Bothwell saw John Elliot of Park often known by the name Wee Jock of the Park riding near Kershopfoot, Bothwell aimed his *dag* (pistol) and shot Elliot from his horse.

Elliott fell wounded to the ground and for a time didn't move; Bothwell thought that he'd killed Elliot, so he progressed to where the body was. Elliot, who wasn't dead, then fought with and stabbed Bothwell with his knife, wounding him, so seriously that he had to be taken back to Hermitage on a litter.

To add insult to injury, for Bothwell, a group of Elliotts had taken over the Castle and Bothwell then had to negotiate to get the Castle back. How that went down in Edinburgh in not recorded, although I think it wouldn't be too well. The action by Elliot give rise to the verse and the motto of the Elliots with the following line:

"My name is Little Jock Elliot, and wha daur meddle wi' me!"

Union of the Crowns and Ill Week

After a reign lasting forty-four years, Queen Elizabeth died. It had long been expected as the Queen had been in ill health for some time and had not married so there was no direct heir. The nearest relative was James VI of Scotland, son of Elizabeth's ill-fated cousin Mary Queen of Scots. James had long since favoured the Union of the Crowns and the English throne and had steered a very careful course to make sure that he achieved it.

When her death was announced on 24 March 1603, Sir Robert Carey was already in the saddle with a ring given from James VI to Elizabeth given to Sir Robert by his sister Philadelphia, Lady Scrope who was one of Elizabeth's ladies in waiting. He took sixty hours and three horses to ride from London to Edinburgh to bring James VI the news that he was now King of a Great Britain. The reign of the Tudors was over; the reign of the Stuarts had just begun.

The reivers on both sides knew this was the end of their way of life; King James had been no friend to the reivers on the Scottish side. There was no indication that he would be any different to the reivers on the English side now that the crowns had been unified.

So it was that the death of a Queen started the most severe week of raiding the borders had known. Reiving and raiding had been on the increase for some years in the latter part of the sixteenth century, with the wardens powerless to stop it. The week after Elizabeth's death would be forever known as "Ill Week" or "Busy Week".

The Earl of Cumbria naturally blamed the raiding on the Cumbrian Grahams, living on the edge of the Debatable Land. However other notable families ran fast and loose during this time, Armstrongs, Elliots, Crosiers, Robsons and Charltons all made the best of the time. Over 4,000 cattle and 5,000 sheep and goats were reived during this one week. One could imagine the Robsons travelling north across the Border to take the Elliot cattle. The Armstongs would be heading south over the Border to remove Charlton and Robson cattle. It does paint an interesting picture of thieves stealing from thieves.

Formerkland Tower near umfries, typical of a 16th century Scottish Tower House.

m a raid on this week; it is thought that the raids stretched as far south as Richmond in North Yorkshire. In the West Marches, the Scottish reivers went as far south as Penrith and Kendal.

Not only did they reive, but they settled old scores with many a murder committed, for they knew the end was in sight.

Pacification of the Borders and End of the Reivers

All in the borders knew what to expect, the marches were disbanded together with the wardens. No longer did James want it to be called the borders but in 1605 he renamed them "the Middle Shires". James had moved south to London with undue haste, with a large entourage of Scots to claim the throne. With some haste and never a friend of the reivers, James set in motion "the Pacification of the Borders".

A number of the more prominent families in the borders realised what was happening and sided with James in effect to become "poacher turned gamekeeper". Amongst those was Sir Robert Ker of Cessford, who had travelled south with James and would sit on the committee that oversaw the Union. Another was George Home, 1st Earl of Dunbar, whom James placed in charge of the pacification of the borders. Courts were set up in border towns and noted reivers and most likely a few other troublemakers were hanged without trial in what became known as "Jeddart Justice" after the town of Jedburgh often called Jeddart. The lower classes of Reivers where hanged at places like the capon tree, a large oak on the south side of Jedburgh. Multiple hangings and drowning during this time were common place. No family was left untouched, with special attention paid to the Grahams, Armstrongs, Elliots and other notable names.

Hangings were not the only way that reivers were dealt with, the good folk of Cumberland all contributed to the exile of the Grahams, who were rounded up and put on a ship to Roscommon in Ireland, to the new Protestant plantation. However being always resourceful, the Grahams changed their name to Maharg and then came back to the borders. Later more of them came back as Grahams; indeed they still inhabit the borders today. Another method of removing troublesome Reivers was to ship them to the

Low Countries to fight in regiments in the Netherlands, against Spanish rule.

James didn't stop with the hanging of people, he ordered the destruction of some forty fortified houses in the borders owned by notable reivers, including Mangerton home of Sim "the laird" Armstrong.

By 1620 the pacification was all but complete and the borders fell in line with the rest of the country. However small bands of Reivers still persisted in living the old way, these were called "moss troopers" and they continued their ways until the late seventeenth century when highwaymen took over the mantle.

The reivers however have left their legacy on the world, both in the words that they have had included in the English language and dictionary such as bereaved, blackmail and gang are all derived from or are words used during that period of our history. Their descendants have also made their mark. The Elliots became noted military commanders and statesmen, the Grahams became evangelists with some irony, the Charltors, Robsons and Milburn's became noted on the football field. The ultimate accolade is probably with the Armstrongs who, after the pacification, were left as a hedeless family, they rode by moonlight and an Armstrong was the first man to walk on the moon. The Reiver families who settled in Ireland moved into Northern Ireland and then to America. Out of the first twelve presidents of the United States, six were descended from Ulster Scots and ultimately the border reivers.

Armstrongs Goodnight

I'll leave the last words in the book to the reivers themselves, in fact to an Armstrong who it is said composed this poem on the night in 1605 before he was due to be hanged in Edinburgh for his part in the murder of Sir John Carmichael the West March Warden in 1600. The poem known as *Armstong's Goodnight*, was presented in Sir Walter Scotts Minstrelsy of The Scottish Borders. Today it is often called *The Parting Glass*.

This night is my parting night,
For here nae langer must I stay;
There's neither friend nor foe o' mine,
But wishes me away.

What I have done thro' lack of wit,
I never can recall;
I hope ye're a' my friends as yet;
Goodnight and joy be with you all!

The Capon tree at Jedburgh. Situated just south of the town and off the A68. This old oak tree was used to as a hanging tree in Reiving times.

Mangerton Tower, Home of Sym "The Laird" Armstrong. The tower was destroyed during the pacification of the borders.

Glossary

Arquebus An early sixteenth century smooth bored musket, one of the first type to have a trigger mechanism, the trigger would fire either a flintlock or a wheel lock. They were less in use towards the end of the sixteenth century.

Arrow Slits Slits in the walls of a fortified structure to fire either a long bow or crossbow from. The long bow arrow slits normally being vertical and the crossbow being horizontal in construction.

Bailey The outer part of a castle, enclosed by the curtain wall. The inside of the bailey would be the outer ward.

Bartizan Overhanging turret on a castle or tower, often containing a stairway to higher floors, used as a watchtower.

Barbican A tower in a castle situated over the gatehouse or a bridge on the entrance to the castle. Can also be a dual tower type gatehouse.

Barmkin Outer wall that surrounds a fortified tower. Normally made from the same material as the tower itself and used as the first line of defence.

Bastle Fortified two-storey house often built by farmers, where the ground floor is vaulted and is used to protect livestock during a raid. Living quarters were on the first floor and were reached by a ladder that could be retracted during a raid.

Bereaved To be relieved of your goods by reivers, later to mean to have lost a loved one.

Bill Hook A curved blade of about thirty centimetres in length and ten centimetres wide with a wooden handle, generally made of ash. Used originally as an agricultural tool for cutting corn. Later it was used as a fighting weapon.

Blackmail (Blackmeale) Illegal rent paid for protection money, 'Meale' was the Scottish word for rent so it became the word for illegal rent.

Burgonet Open faced steel helmet with a peak at the front, like the Morion helmet it often had a comb on the top to deflect blows.

Buttery A room in a castle used for the storage of provisions to feed the occupants of the castle. Often built onto the outside curtain wall.

Caltrop (Caltrap) Three or four pronged iron star sharpened to points that was used spread on the ground to cripple horses or other tracking animals.

Cleugh A deep ravine or valley in the landscape.

Cold Trod Pursuit of reivers by the person relieved of their goods within six days of the theft.

Crenellate Licence to The royal permission normally issued on parchment for an owner to fortify a manor house by the addition of battlements.

Crenellation (Castellation) The pattern of raised stones on the top of a parapet walls of a castle to assist the defenders.

Crossbow A bow mounted horizontally on a wooden stock, the string being drawn back with either a lever or a wheel and pulley. Very accurate and powerful weapon but slow to reload and fire the bolt or quarrel.

Dagg Small smooth bored early pistols, either flintlock or Wheelock.

Debateable Land The unmarked and untamed land on the England-Scotland Border, finally divided in 1552 by the French Ambassador.

Donjon Early name for the keep in a castle. Usually contained the living quarters of the family and servants.

Gavelkind A will where the estate of the dead person is equally divided between the deceased sons.

Grayne Another name for the family in the borders. To go with the grayne was to go with your family.

Halberd A five or six foot long pole with an axehead on top, combined with a spear-point at 90 degrees to the axe. Much used during the early part of the sixteenth century and at the battle of Flodden.

Handfasting The act of living together before marriage, whilst waiting for a priest. The period usually lasted a year and any children born during this time would be treated as family even if the couple parted before getting married.

Hot Trod Pursuit of reivers by the person relieved of their goods, starting the same day as the day of the theft, signified by the carrying of a lit torch of peat on a pole to signify the Trod.

Insight The internal goods and chattels of a dwelling such as blankets, rugs, pots and pans. All were often taken in a raid if access to the dwelling was available.

Jack A quilted jacket where the inner and outer layers are stitched together with either small metal or bone pieces in between. This offered protection, but was lighter than armour and more flexible when on horseback for long periods.

Jeddart Justice To be hanged first and sent to trial later, in that there is no Justice.

Latch A small single-handed crossbow used as a personal weapon, much like a pistol.

Merse The fertile land north of the River Tweed in Scotland, the centre in the medieval period of the wool trade for Scotland.

Morion A steel helmet made in either one or two parts and annealed in a forge, popular in Europe during the sixteenth century and into the 17th century. A comb on the top of the helmet was used both as a sign of rank, the higher the comb the higher the rank. The second reason for the cone was to deflect blows directed at the head.

Motte The mound on which the early keep of a castle would be placed, this would be in the central part of the castle with the bailey surrounding it.

Musters A roll call of men and weapons, both in castles of serving soldiers and in the surrounding villages, of able-bodied men who can serve during times of conflict.

Oubliette A dungeon in a castle, usually a cell underground with no light and very little access.

Pele (Peel) Fortified tower house of three or four storeys, often with a beacon holder on the roof. The ground floor is often vaulted and used to store livestock during a raid.

Pennon Knights flag or standard in his own colours, often presented on the end of a lance and taken into battle.

Pike Infantry weapon of the Middle Ages, consisting of a long pole of up to 7.5 metres in length with a spear at the top. Pikemen were often formed into squares or schiltrons to face an enemy.

Poleaxe Combined axe and spear on a long pole similar to the halberd but with the addition of a rear-pointing spike.

Pommel The ball-shaped knob on the hilt of a sword, this could be decorated with the owner's crest, and could be inlaid with precious stones.

Postern A small wooden gate at the rear of a castle, used during a siege to send out scouting parties and messengers. Can be used to bring in food and other relief supplies.

Reiver Person or persons who steal or reive goods from others.

Solar Tower Tower within a castle positioned to get the maximum amount of sun, hence its name. It would often be the living quarters of the lady of the castle.

Slewe Hound Dog, similar to a bloodhound, trained to follow a scent. Often used in the pursuit of reivers on a trod.

Spurs Metal implements worn on riding boots to help control a horse whilst riding.

Yett Iron latticed door that was used as a second barrier behind the main wooden door of a bastle or Tower. The old Scottish word for 'cate'.

Further Reading

Borland, Robert *Border Raids and Reivers*, Oakpast, 2010

Brander, Michael *Tales of the Borders,* Mainstream Publishing, 1991

Durham, Keith *Border Reivers* 1513-1603, Osprey Publishing, 2011

Durham, Keith *Strongholds of the Border Reivers*, Osprey Publishing, 2008

Geldard, Ed *Northumberland Strongholds*, Francis Lincoln, 2009

Grint, Julia *Bastles An Introduction to the Bastle Houses of Northumberland*, Ergo Press, 2008

Grant, Will *Tweeddale,* Oliver & Boyd, 1948

Hamilton, Judy *Scottish Battles,* Geddes & Grosset, 2004

Hugill, Robert *Castles of Cumberland and Westmorland*, Frank Graham, 1977

Hugill, Robert *Borderland Castles and Peles,* Sandhill Press, 1996

MacDonald Fraser, George *The Steel Bonnets*, Pan Books, 1974

Marsden, John *The Illustrated Border Ballads*, MacMillan, 1990

Moffat, Alisdair *The Reivers*, Birlinn, 2010

Moffat, Alisdair *The Borders*, Birlinn, 2007

Nixon, Philip *Exploring Border Reivers History,* Breedon Books, 2007

Trough, DLW *The Last Years of a Frontier*, Sandhill Press, 1987

Watson, Godfrey *The Border Reivers*, Sandhill Press, 1994